Never mind the cobwebs....
HELP ME KILL THIS SPIDER

by
BISHOP GEORGE DAWSON

Never mind the Cobwebs . . . Help Me Kill This Spider!

by Bishop George Dawson

© 2025 Sunday Morning Ministries
dnjgoree@sundaymorningministries.org

All rights reserved. No part of this publication may be reproduced, stored, or transmitted in any form or by any means—electronic, mechanical, photocopying, recording, or otherwise—without prior written permission from the publisher, except for brief quotations used in reviews or scholarly works.

Scripture Quotations
Unless otherwise indicated, all Scripture quotations are taken from the **King James Version of the Bible**.

Graphic Designer
Micah Sanford
micah@wallstreetimage.com

ISBN
Paperback: 978-0-9896602-7-3
Ebook: 978-0-9896602-8-0

To my wife, children, and grandchildren—
you are my heartbeat, my legacy, and my joy in the journey.

To my surviving siblings, Larry and Tammy—
thank you for your steadfast love, prayers, and the bond that time and distance can never break.

To **Cross Tabernacle Church** and **Calvary International Worship Center**—
thank you for standing in faith and walking in vision.

To my mentors and teachers—
your voices trained my ear to hear God,
your example taught me how to walk worthy of the call.

This book is our testimony—
born in prayer, proven in warfare,
and offered back to the One who always wins.

Table of Contents

Forward X

Introduction XVII

Part 1: Power of Divine Order

Chapter 1 - The Ant: Preparation is Prophecy 23

Chapter 2 - The Conies: High Praise that Brings the Glory 30

Chapter 3 - The Locusts: The Power of One Accord 39

Part 2: Deliverance Through Fire

Chapter 4 - The Anointing that Destroys the Yoke 49

Chapter 5 - The Webs: Three Traps of Deception 62

    Funnel Web 63

    Sticky Web 65

    Flat Web 67

Chapter 6 - The Spiders: Exposing Demonic Schemes	74
The Loxosceles Spider: Digging for Destruction	75
The Wolf Spider: Pulpit Predator	78
The Hopping Spider: Spirit of Contamination	82
Th Hati Hati Spider: The Curse of Conditional Praise	85
The Two-Faced Spider: Weaving the Web of Deceit & Contamination	88
The Trap-Door Spider: Silent Devourer of Harvest and Anointing	93
Recluse Spider: Poison in the Cracks of Complacency	98
The Black Widow: Destroying Within	103
The Tarantula: The Battle of the Mind	113
Chapter 7 - My Testimony	124

Forward

I have heard George Dawson preach many times over the years. As always, his messages are filled with *prophetic revelation*, which edifies any hungry soul searching for direction, destiny, and the dialectic. His prophetic office has blessed thousands over the years. Now, the Lord has given Dawson a **divine assignment** — to author one of the most profound literary works I have ever read.

I found this book to be **enlightening**, as it exposes the works of darkness and reveals how the inner workings of schemes, traps, and snares are strategically woven together in any life whose faith is fixated across time and place. The battleground for the cognitive, according to Dawson, is a primary place of contest and competition, where these strategies have found success in numbing the importunity of the will.

However, this is no secret, as Scripture forewarns believers to *fight the good fight of faith, to war as good soldiers, and to be strong in the Lord and in the power of His might*. Yet, in this book, he illustrates these traps cleverly by using insects and small creatures, showing how *the power of their natures can usurp and control a life unbeknownst to reality.*

There is a part of the book that explains the types of spiders and how each of these is effective in faith-killing. Each species has a specific characteristic in its nature that is used to impart dangerous and lethal attacks, which, if the believer is not vigilant, could easily lead to the very outcome these strategies intended.

Readers become aware of the impact spiders have in their habitat, but removing a spider from its web and transporting it to a life-inhabiting faith to break down explains the number of diseased and sickly narratives reported today in the Christian church. *Sick marriages, broken relationships, loneliness, lack of self-respect, gift interruptions, corrupted thoughts, blessings turned to curses, withheld seeds*—these are but a sampling of how spiders can reverse progress and trap faith in cycles of insanity.

The reader, however, is not to be left undone! Dawson's prophetic insight kicks into high gear on how to prevent these spiders from taking over.

There is hope after each spider attempts to destroy.

There is joy after each spider's cover is blown.

There is faith after each spider's inability to cope with the light.

Dawson refuses to let any reader travel lightly through these pages. Every bag must be packed to the brim to find success against any insect, creature, or spider that will attempt to use its power — but will ultimately fail.

This book addresses warfare in which *ignorance is not a premium*, and the reader must be kept abreast of reality.

But that is not how this story ends. After reading this, the soon-to-be best-selling book should leave every son and daughter of faith feeling ecstatic about **victorious living — a life that cannot be killed, stolen, or destroyed.**

~ Bishop Richard D. Howell Jr.

. . .

There comes a time in everyone's life when the dust settles, the noise quiets, and you finally notice the cobwebs—those delicate signs of neglect that have crept into the corners of your heart, your home, or your spirit. Most of us reach for a broom and call it progress. But this book reminds us of a more profound truth: *sometimes the problem isn't the cobwebs at all — it's the spider still spinning them.*

Never Mind the Cobwebs, Help Me Kill This Spider isn't just a catchy title; *it's a prayer, a declaration, and a wake-up call.* It invites us to stop pretending that surface cleaning will fix what's broken. Instead, it challenges us to confront the root of the problem — the habits, fears, relationships, or mindsets that keep weaving the same tangled mess, no matter how often we try to clean it up.

With equal parts humor, honesty, and holy conviction, this book peels back the layers of life's clutter to reveal a simple but powerful truth:

Lasting change begins when we stop managing symptoms and start surrendering sources.

It's about courage — *the courage to say,* "Lord, I'm done dusting. Show me the spider."

If you've ever felt stuck in cycles that won't break, if you've ever prayed for peace but kept finding yourself tangled again, then you're in the right place. This book isn't about perfection; it's about *pursuit*. It's not about pretending the cobwebs don't bother you — it's about *trusting God enough to go after what's causing them.*

So, take a breath. Put down your broom. Open your heart.

Because what you're holding isn't just another inspirational read…

It's an invitation to freedom.

Bishop George Evens Dawson, Jr. is one of this generation's *most influential and sought-after men of God*. Millions have been delivered and received salvation through the ministry God has gifted him. His *spiritual insight and intellectual prowess* are precisely what the world needs in this hour — **to prepare us for the return of our Lord and Savior, Jesus Christ!**

~ *Pastor Arcenia Richards, Jr.*

…

Every so often, God raises up a voice that doesn't just preach truth—it *pierces through the noise* and calls the Body back to the altar. My brother and friend, Bishop George Dawson, is one of those voices. His ministry has always carried a *rare combination of revelation and relevance, conviction and compassion.*

In this book, **Never Mind the Cobwebs**, he delivers not just a message, but a **mantle** — *a call to personal revival and spiritual maintenance* for those who dare to carry the oil.

After reading part of the manuscript, I was deeply moved by how **practical and prophetic** Bishop Dawson's message is. With the heart of a pastor and the insight of a seasoned watchman, he exposes how *spiritual decay begins—not with sudden failure, but with small neglects.* He reminds us that it's not the cobwebs that destroy the flow; it's the spider that built them. *You can shout, sweep, and sing all day long, but until you deal with the source, the webs will keep returning.*

As I read, I was struck by how vividly Bishop Dawson brings truth to life. The ant, the cony, the locust, and finally the spider—all reveal wisdom from the small things. And through this revelation, he brings us to the heart of **spiritual stewardship:**

The anointing must be guarded. The oil must stay pure. The fire must stay hot.

Bishop Dawson reminds us that *you cannot keep spoiled oil and expect fresh fire.* The same anointing that draws God's presence can, if left uncovered, begin to attract decay. Through his own experiences and the unfiltered wisdom of the Holy Spirit, he shows us what happens when we delay fixing what's broken in our hearts, homes, and ministries. **He doesn't write from theory—he writes from testimony.**

What I love most about this work is that it doesn't leave you in despair; it points you toward **deliverance.** It reminds you that *the power of God's anointing still destroys every yoke.* It's a call to **restoration**—to repair the holes, rekindle the fire, and recover the fragrance of fresh oil.

This book is not just a teaching—it's a **tool.** It's a *mirror for the minister, a warning for the worker, and a wake-up call for the worshiper.* If you have ever felt the weight of ministry, if you have ever sensed the dullness that comes when your flame begins to fade, let this message grip your spirit.

To my brother, Bishop George Dawson—thank you for writing what many have felt but few have dared to articulate. You have given the Church *not just a word, but a way back to purity, power, and passion.*

To every reader—*don't just read this book, live it*. Let the Holy Ghost reveal the spiders hiding in the corners of your life. Fix the holes. Protect your oil. And **keep your fire burning so hot that no web can ever form again.**

Bishop James Edwell

...

There comes a time in every generation when **God raises up a sound**—a divine harmony that calls His people out of isolation and into alignment. *Never Mind the Cobwebs: Help Me Kill This Spider* is a **clarion call** to that sound. It's not just a book—it's a **revelation of divine strategy** for those who are ready to move from scattered strength to **unstoppable unity**.

The Spirit of the Lord has always moved most powerfully where there is **agreement**. From the upper room in Acts 2 to the mighty armies of Israel, God's glory is most revealed when His people move as one. The locust, though small and seemingly insignificant, carries a principle that the modern Church desperately needs to recover—the **law of harmony**. It's not the strength of one, but the **submission of many** that releases the power of heaven on earth.

This book invites readers to **rediscover the sacred rhythm of spiritual harmony.** You will learn that **preparation without unity is powerless,** and **protection without obedience is incomplete.** Like the locusts that "have no king, yet go they forth all of them by bands" (Proverbs 30:27), God is teaching us that **authority is not always visible—but order is always vital.**

In these pages, Bishop George Dawson captures our attention and reminds us that **every connection carries a sound, and every circle creates a cycle.** The **wrong alignment can silence** your destiny, but the **right one can amplify your anointing.** This is more than poetic truth—it's **prophetic instruction.** When God wants to shift your life, He'll often start by **adjusting your circle.**

Never Mind the Cobwebs reveals that **separation is not always rejection—it's preparation.** Unity sometimes requires **pruning.** Just as Abram could not hear God until Lot departed, some voices and relationships must be released before heaven can reveal its next instruction.

Through wisdom, personal testimony, and revelation, you'll encounter the **balance of faith and discernment— understanding that faith has no substitute for wisdom.** It's a message that challenges us to move beyond emotional zeal and into **spiritual precision.** The true test of maturity is not how high you can shout, but how well you can **stay in rhythm with the will of God.**

The locusts move together not because they are **forced— but because they are focused.** And when the Church learns that kind of unity—when pastors, leaders, families, and saints begin to **march in one sound**—the atmosphere itself must change.

My prayer is that as you read this book, you will **hear beyond the words and catch the sound of the Spirit.** That you will feel the **stirring of divine agreement rising within you.** That you will say, *"Lord, make me part of the band."*

May this revelation empower you to **align with the right people, move in divine order, and operate under the unstoppable grace of one accord.**

Together we rise, together we move, and together—we win.

~Bishop T. David Dockery Sr.

Introduction

Every preacher has a moment when a message doesn't just visit—it grabs hold and won't let go. I had that moment years ago in Jackson, Mississippi. I was a young preacher—*new shoes, trembling hands*—invited to speak at Apostle William Bonner's church. Every night, before service, we prayed, and every night, the assistant pastor would close with the same line: *"Lord, remove the cobwebs."*

But on that fifth night, while we were still on our knees, an elderly church mother pressed her way to the altar. She laid her hand on his back and said, with the wisdom of heaven itself: **"Lord, it ain't the cobwebs—kill the spider."** That sentence changed everything. It opened my eyes to the truth: too many of us are busy sweeping at cobwebs—the *surface problems*—when the real issue is the **spider that made them.** We rebuke the fruit but never deal with the root. We patch what shows, but we never touch what hides. And **every habit, every cycle, every thought you ignore is a choice to remain in bondage.** *What you are not changing, you are choosing.*

This revelation became the foundation of this book. It's not just a sermon—it's a **spiritual strategy for your life.** Through Proverbs 30:24–28, we will study four small creatures—*ants, conies, locusts, and the spider*—that God

Himself calls **"exceeding wise."** Each one carries a revelation that, if applied, will transform your life from the inside out.

The Ants teach preparation. They store food in the summer so they don't starve in the winter. Spiritually, this is about **preparing in faith, storing up prayer, wisdom, and discipline in anticipation of trials.** Apply this, and you will walk into seasons of blessings ready, confident, and equipped for God's plan. When the storms hit, you won't stumble—you'll rise.

From preparation flows protection. **The Conies teach protection.** Weak as they may seem, they build their homes in the rocks. That's you—*weak in the world, strong in the Rock.* You'll learn to dwell in Christ, the refuge, and avoid the snakes in the valleys of life. **Weakness in the right place is stronger than strength in the wrong place.** When you build on the Rock, you will survive what others fall to.

And where protection meets preparation, **unity becomes a powerful force.** The Locusts teach unity. They have no king, yet they move in coordinated bands. That's the power of **obedience without pride, humility without compromise.** Apply this to your family, your church, your ministry—and doors will open that you never imagined. You will be unstoppable when you move in unity with God and others.

Finally comes the hardest lesson: **the spider teaches perseverance and purpose.** The spider represents the **root**

problems in your life—the habits, the cycles, the sins, the spiritual attacks that keep recurring. Confront the spider, and the cobwebs will no longer control your home, your heart, or your destiny.

I want to share something important, and it is essential to understand: Proverbs 30, written by **Prince Agur, a man who loved his mother dearly.** I see myself in him—growing up under the care of a *strong, loving mother*, alongside my little sister Tammy, facing struggles and storms together. Our older siblings had ruined our father's credit, and we learned to survive through it all. There were times we scraped *cockroaches out of cornflakes to eat*. Poverty, struggle, and trials were real—but so was the **power of God to transform our lives.** This message brought my sister and me out of the ghetto, and it can do the same for you.

When you let these lessons sink into your spirit, you will begin to see things differently. You will stop living in the same cycles. You will **prepare your faith, protect your heart, move in unity, and face the hidden forces holding you back.** Your family will be shielded. Your mind will be clear. Your spirit will rise.

Get ready to see a **breakthrough.** Get ready to walk in the **freedom** you've only dreamed about. Get ready to confront the spider in your life—and when you do, your testimony will shake the heavens.

Never mind the cobwebs, Child of God. It's time to **get the spider.** Once the spider is gone, you will walk in **power, purpose, and blessings like never before.**

Part One:

The Power of Divine Order

Step into the Seasons God Has Ordained for You

Chapter 1

The Ants: Preparation is Prophecy

The ants are a people not strong, yet they prepare their meat in the summer.

Proverbs 30:25

Now and then, God hides a great truth in something small. He'll tuck a mighty revelation inside a tiny creature to see who's humble enough to learn from it. And when you open your Bible to Proverbs 30:25, you meet the ant—small, easily overlooked, but **supremely strategic**. The ant knows the time. She doesn't wait until the winter snows fall to get ready; she moves while the sun is shining, she works while the ground is soft, and she prepares while others are distracted or playing. That's the wisdom of the ant: she understands that every season has a purpose, and what you gather in the heat determines if you survive the cold. **The message is clear:** *Stay ready so you don't have to get ready.*

You are not working without direction, Child of God. Your preparation is merely aligning yourself with the future God has already promised. The Lord declares in,

> *"For I know the plans I have for you," declares the Lord, "plans to prosper you and not to harm you, plans to give you hope and a future."*
>
> Jeremiah 29:11

Your act of preparation is the prophetic evidence that you believe the promise is already on its way; you are building the barn to hold the harvest that is certain to come.

That's where many of us struggle. We want the full blessing and the shouted harvest, but the blessing is tied to timing and movement. The ant doesn't complain when it's hot; she uses the heat to build for what's coming. There is a season to gather and a season to grow,

> *To every thing there is a season, and a time to every purpose under the heaven:*
>
> Ecclesiastes 3:1

The ant doesn't fight the season; she flows with it, taking what God gives her and making it enough.

The Purpose of Rain

We serve a sovereign God who sits on the throne and orchestrates every moment. The prophet Daniel reminds us,

And he changeth the times and the seasons: he removeth kings, and setteth up kings: he giveth wisdom unto the wise, and knowledge to them that know understanding.

Daniel 2:21

If God controls the times and seasons—if He is the one who sets the stage—then our job is to be found ready, walking in the wisdom He has already provided.

You cannot despise what different seasons bring. Rain seems inconvenient, an interruption to your sunny day, but the Bible itself stresses its necessity. In the book of Joel, the prophet declares

Be glad then, ye children of Zion, and rejoice in the LORD your God: for he hath given you the former rain moderately, and he will cause to come down for you the rain, the former rain, and the latter rain in the first month.

Joel 2:23

This scripture reveals God's purpose in the seasons. The former rain hits the dry, hard ground to make it tender—ready to be seeded, easy to plant. God wants your heart to be tender and ready to receive the Word; only then can you bear fruit. The latter rain, which comes in the spring, is designed to make the fruit fat and acceptable for harvest. **God is economical! He wastes no trial, no situation, no tribulation.** It is either the former rain, to prepare your soul to receive, or the latter rain, to make you wiser, better, and your fruit acceptable. You get ready now—because faith prepares while fear procrastinates.

I remember talking with a woman years ago who had lost her job. She was hurting, scared, and ready to give up. She told me, "Bishop, I don't know what to do. I'm just waiting on the right time."

I looked at her and asked, "Sis, what's in your hands?"

She hesitated, then said softly, "All I know how to do is bake."

And I told her, "Then **bake your way out.**"

That word lit something in her spirit. She stopped waiting for the perfect season and started working on her portion, selling cakes to neighbors and pies to friends at church. Before long, she had a full storefront bakery. When she stopped waiting for perfection and started working on her portion, God breathed on her preparation. **God multiplies movement, not excuses.** We love to shout about the blessing, but God only blesses what's ready. Preparation is the proof of faith.

Preparation Demands Sacrifice

However, the Ant's wisdom demands a more profound truth: **Preparation isn't just about stocking the barn; it's about renovating the vessel.** You can't walk in a new anointing with an old appetite. When wine ages, it grows richer, stronger, and more potent, but the blessing requires a renewed vessel. You can't pour the blessing into an empty schedule, a distracted mind, or an unready spirit. The truth is that the vessel cannot be truly filled because the flesh still occupies it. That's why the Word says,

> *In this flesh dwelleth no good thing.*
> *Romans 7:18*

Something in you has to die for something greater to live. The old habits of the flesh must be crucified—the old ways of thinking, the patterns of doubt, worry, and negativity. Paul declares,

> *And they that are Christ's have crucified the flesh with the affections and lusts.*
> *Galatians 5:24*

This is where many of us fail. We pick up the cross, but we leave the **affections and lusts in a spiritual luggage** on the ground, only to pick them up later. We stop committing the sin, but we keep the desire for the sin. True preparation demands that the affections and lusts be crucified right alongside the flesh, or you will always have fleshly challenges and issues. Preparation is the silent, difficult work of letting go of those affections. **Before God can fill you with power, purpose, and blessings like never before, He's got to free you.** What is the purpose of this freedom and renovation? The Apostle Paul prays,

> *And to know the love of Christ that surpasses knowledge, that you may be filled with all the fullness of God.*
>
> *Ephesians 3:19*

When you surrender the old, heaven releases the new and calls us to be filled to the full.

Child of God, you can shout, you can dance, you can declare all you want—but if you don't prepare, you'll miss what you prayed for. You can't pour the blessing into a vessel that is still occupied by the flesh. This is the hour to build your faith while the sun is still shining. **Store up prayer, store up praise, store up the Word.** When the test hits, it'll be too late to start praying; your victory depends on the faith you prepared in peace. So I'm telling you—start preparing right now. Build what you've been delaying. Write what you've been afraid to start. Because when you move in faith before the season changes, God meets you in power when it does. **Get ready! The same God who gives the harvest is the God who honors preparation.**

The Ant's Prayer of Preparation

Father, I thank You for the wisdom of the ant. Teach me to move before I see, to trust before I touch, and to prepare before the promise shows up. Break every lazy spirit, every fearful hesitation, every excuse that keeps me unready for Your move.

Lord, help me to build now—to store prayer, to study Your Word, to walk in discipline. Let me not be distracted by comfort or delay, but recognize that seasons shift suddenly, and I must be found faithful. Father, crucify my flesh and kill the old appetite that resists change. Renew my mind, strengthen my hands, and position my heart to receive the harvest You've already ordained.

I declare: this is my season to prepare, my season to build, my season to believe! *And when the rain falls, I'll be ready to receive it. In Jesus' mighty name—Amen!*

Chapter 2

The Conies:

High Praise that Brings the Glory

The conies are but a feeble folk, yet make they their houses in the rocks.

Proverbs 30:26

After the Ant teaches you to **prepare**—to store up and adjust for the coming season—the Lord immediately introduces the second lesson: **positioning**.

It is not enough to simply *have* the blessing; you must be correctly positioned to keep it. Knowing correct positioning is the wisdom of the **Conies**. They are a feeble folk—small, weak, and vulnerable—but they make their houses in the **rocks**. They have found the secret to survival: **Elevation**.

The Conies teach us a life-saving truth: **weakness in the right place is stronger than strength in the wrong place.** When you are feeble, you must stop seeking comfort in the world and start seeking refuge in the **Rock**. That Rock is Christ, and He is the only place where the venom of the enemy cannot reach you.

The Danger of the Low Place

The Conies understand one fundamental truth: **I cannot survive the valley.**

If you choose to stay in the low places, the flatlands of your spirit and your life, you automatically choose to live with the enemy. And what thrives in the valley? **Snakes.**

Snakes are drawn to low places. They represent the spirit of **jealousy, bitterness, and poison.** They are the people, the habits, and the spirits that operate with the intent to bite, to squeeze, and to destroy. **There is a high cost of low living.** You cannot dwell in the valley and expect victory! The scripture declares a divine economy in Romans 6:23:

> *For the wages of sin is death; but the gift of God is eternal life through Jesus Christ our Lord.*

Child of God, when you look at that paycheck of sin, you realize you are getting paid in *death*. Your Father has an inheritance waiting for you. It is time to **strike on hell for higher wages**! What you are not changing, you are choosing.

The Conies teach us that the higher you go in your faith, your praise, and your worship, the fewer of those snakes you will see. When your **faith** is high, the atmosphere of fear cannot breathe. When your **praise** is high, the conditions are no longer conducive to the snake's survival. When you elevate your **worship**, you change the atmosphere of the battleground.

The Snake in the Palace

The most dangerous snake is the one you bring into your own house.

I remember the story of a young boy who brought home a beautiful snake. His mother warned him, "Get rid of it," but the boy hid it in his room. It was attractive—maybe it had diamonds on its back—but the mother knew the truth: **It is a snake, and its nature is to bite.**

The snake, over time, got comfortable. It wrapped around the boy, and he thought it was just affection. He mistook the squeeze for **comfort**. One day, the snake bit him.

Even more chilling is the true story of the woman and her pet python. She thought her snake was sick because it stopped eating and would stretch out to her entire length, then wrap itself around her every night. She, too, mistook the squeeze for **comfort**. She took her beloved pet to the vet, expecting a diagnosis, but the vet delivered a prophetic terror: **The snake was not sick; it was meticulously measuring her body, refusing food to make space for the massive meal it was preparing for!** It was not finding comfort in her; it was sizing her up.

That is how the enemy works. That snake is bold enough to **join the church, beg for a title, gain a position, and spend months measuring you up so they can devour you.** The snake gets close enough to eat you alive. The people closest to you are not always ready for your story because they cannot handle your **glory**. They do not want to pray for you; they want to prey on you.

The snake is poisonous, and its bite reminds me of the mega-church challenge: just because they are big doesn't mean they are right. The snake's poison doesn't hurt right away—it hurts two or three days later, and then you start to swell. **That swelling is not growth; it's an infection.** It is the venom of spiritual compromise and misaligned leadership that puffs up but never produces life.

The Mountain: A Matter of Dimension

If you want to survive the snake, you have to move to the Conies' altitude. When you make your house in the Rock, you are declaring that your safety is not in your strength, but in your Savior. The Rock is not just a dwelling place; it is a **praise position**. As the Psalmist said:

> *For in the time of trouble he shall hide me in his pavilion: in the secret of his tabernacle shall he hide me; he shall set me up upon a rock.*
>
> Psalm 27:5

God called Moses to Mount Sinai. God's presence was revealed there.

> *¹²And the LORD said unto Moses, Come up to me into the mount, and be there: and I will give thee tables of stone, and a law, and commandments which I have written; that thou mayest teach them. ¹³And Moses rose up, and his minister Joshua: and Moses went up into the mount of God. ¹⁴And he said unto the elders, Tarry ye here for us, until we come again unto you: and, behold, Aaron and Hur are with you: if any man have any matters to do, let him come unto them. ¹⁵And Moses went up into the mount, and a cloud covered the mount. ¹⁶And the glory of the LORD abode upon mount Sinai, and the cloud covered it six days: and the seventh day he called unto Moses out of the midst of the cloud. ¹⁷And the sight of the glory of the LORD was like devouring fire on the top of the mount in the eyes of the children of Israel. ¹⁸And*

Moses went into the midst of the cloud, and gat him up into the mount: and Moses was in the mount forty days and forty nights.

Exodus 24: 12-18

The elders ascended to the center of the mountain, but **Moses alone** made it to the top. At that summit, snakes are forbidden. Why? Because the snake is a creature of the low earth, it cannot survive in the rarefied air of the heights. In this instance, the "snakes" cannot handle the **glory of God**.

Every spiritual type corresponds to a different **dimension of authority**. These dimensions have doors. When God opens a new dimension for you, the old enemy that chased you in the valley cannot handle the spiritual **altitude** you are standing on. The glory of God intensifies with each dimension. Therefore, the pastor of the church must dwell in this **glory**, a dimension where the enemy cannot reach him. The pastor must live at a level that allows him to see Jesus clearly, to hear Him, and to protect the flock with the **anointing** of that altitude. His life must be wholly conducive to the glory.

You can see this truth in the wilderness: while Moses was on the mountaintop, the congregation down below made the golden calf—and that's where the serpents and judgment had access. **Levels have setbacks, but dimensions have doors.** Joshua, who followed Moses until the end, learned to walk in both the low and high places, and at the end of his life declared,

> *Now therefore fear the Lord, and serve him in sincerity and in truth: and put away the gods which your fathers served on the other side of the flood, and in Egypt; and serve ye the Lord.*
>
> Joshua 24:14

He made the high position permanent.

Your Weapon is Praise

The snake that exalts itself against you is a stronghold, and you cannot fight it in your own flesh. If this snake is bold enough to measure you up, you need a different weapon. Our spiritual weaponry is not carnal:

> *For the weapons of our warfare are not carnal, but mighty through God to the pulling down of strong holds; Casting down imaginations, and every high thing that exalteth itself against the knowledge of God, and bringing into captivity every thought to the obedience of Christ.*
>
> 2 Corinthians 10:4-5

The praises found within the scriptures in Hebrew are your mighty weapons. First, there is **Yadah**, which is the physical extension of your hands in an act of gratitude, dependence, and **surrender**. Then there is **Towdah**, expressing gratitude through an offering or sacrifice. You must also employ **Shabach**, which is to shout praise in a loud, joyous way—a confidence that **disorients the enemy**. Finally, **Halal**—to clap your hands and shout Hallelujah—is the sound that **freezes the enemy** in its tracks, securing your **deliverance**.

Your praise must always remain in high altitudes. When you lift your hands (*Yadah*), you are establishing the Rock's border. When you lift your voice (*Shabach*), you are changing the elevation of your battle. The Conies teach you to climb and to hold your position, no matter the storm below. Your endurance in the Rock is proof that you refuse to be poisoned by the enemy's tactics.

Prayer: A High Altitude Declaration

*Father, I thank You for the wisdom of the **Conies**. I declare today that I am a feeble folk, and I refuse to live in the valleys where the enemy thrives. Lead me to the **Rock of my salvation** and teach me to dwell in the high places.*

I repent for living low, for mistaking the squeeze for comfort, and for ignoring the venomous nature of the snakes in my life. Give me the discernment to recognize jealousy, and the spiritual strength to separate myself from anyone or anything that is committed to my destruction. Show me, reveal to me the intentions of those around me.

*Lord, I use the weapons of my warfare right now! I lift my hands in **Yadah**, I shout my confidence in **Shabach**, and I give You my **Towdah** sacrifice. I declare my praise is ascending to the high altitude, and I claim my **deliverance** from the low-living spirit!*

*I refuse to be bound; I choose the **high dimension of Your presence**! I declare my house is built upon the Rock, and **I am free to serve You as You intended.** In Jesus' mighty name—Amen!*

Chapter 3

The Locusts:

The Power of One Accord

The locusts have no king, yet go they forth all of them by bands.

Proverbs 30:27

You have learned to *prepare* (The Ant) and to *protect your position* (The Conies). Now, the third lesson deals with the unstoppable, climate-changing force of **Unity**.

The locust is feeble alone. It is a simple insect that is easily crushed. But the Scripture declares that, despite having no central leader, they go forth all of them in bands. This is a prophetic revelation: even without a visible king, the power of agreement creates an overwhelming, irresistible force. They move in one accord.

If you are going to walk in true power—the kind of power that shifts spiritual and natural climates and secures your deliverance—you must recognize that **submission and obedience must work in perfect harmony.** You must possess a foundational level of obedience to God to harmonize with your brothers and sisters and move as one, in a sound body.

The reason the locusts are so terrifying is their unity. They move with total, shared purpose. There is no jealousy, no competition, and no comparison in a swarm of locusts. They move in destructive, unified power. When you operate with the people God has placed in your life—your family, your church, your ministry—you cease to be a nuisance and become an unstoppable, sovereign force.

The Word commands this harmony:

> *Complete my joy by being of the same mind, having the same love, being in full accord and of one mind. Do nothing out of selfish ambition or vain conceit, but in humility consider others better than yourselves.*
>
> *Philippians 2:2–3*

The Locust teaches you that true power is not found in strength, but in **the humility of submission** that allows the collective to achieve one sound.

The best human example of this law of harmony is the husband and wife. They are designed to function in divine rhythm. When one member of the household is out of sync with the others, the entire household feels it. The atmosphere becomes divided, the blessing becomes delayed, and the flow of peace is disrupted. When the marriage is out of tune, the entire family loses its melody.

This is why the Apostle Paul warns,

> *A little leaven leaveneth the whole lump.*
> *Galatians 5:9*

It's true—the old saying stands: *One bad apple spoils the bunch.* A single note of pride, jealousy, or rebellion can spoil the entire corporate sound. You are not meant to face life's obstacles alone. God has placed people around you—a *band*—to ensure your survival and victory. If you refuse to align, you refuse the power of the Locust.

Circles and Cycles

But hear me—**whoever is in your circle creates your cycle.** If you keep finding yourself in the same destructive cycle, you need to check your circle. There's somebody in that band that's throwing the sound off. Some people are not assigned to your next level—they're only comfortable in your last one.

There comes a moment when you must have what I call a *cut-off ministry*. That doesn't mean you stop loving people—it means you stop letting them limit you. **says,**

> *He removes kings and sets up new ones.*
>
> Daniel 2:21

Some people, God is waiting on *you* to remove. Until you do, He can't replace them with who belongs in your next season.

Every relationship carries a sound. Every connection produces a cycle. And some cycles will keep repeating until you decide to end the song. Don't let misplaced loyalty silence your destiny. **Some blessings are for your eyes only.** Not everyone can handle what God is preparing for you. That's why sometimes He disguises a thing before He reveals a thing—He hides the blessing until you've released the wrong company.

Remember Abram. In Genesis 12, God told him to go to a land He would show him. But Lot decided to tag along with Abram. And as long as Lot was in his circle, God stopped talking. It wasn't until Genesis 13, when Lot finally departed, that God spoke again. There are some "Lots" in your life—people who mean well but block the flow of revelation. You can't walk in complete harmony carrying people who aren't in rhythm with your assignment.

Sometimes unity requires separation. You've got to remove what's out of tune before you can hear what's divine. When you get your circle right, your cycle will shift. And once your cycle shifts, your whole atmosphere changes.

Faith Is No Substitute for Wisdom

This is where the power of one accord must harmonize with the **wisdom of the Kingdom.**

I remember my first revival as a new pastor. God spoke these words: *"Faith has no substitute for wisdom."* I didn't understand it then. I was in Huntington, West Virginia. The second night, the tent was packed. A Caucasian pastor sat in the back, laughing every night as if I were telling jokes. The Holy Spirit told me, *"Call the man out and prophesy."*

In front of five hundred people, I said, "Sir, you have twin daughters. You have a redheaded daughter, and you have another who is on rock cocaine listening to heavy metal. God will save them both!"

After the service, he brought me to his mansion in the hills. He introduced me to a woman in a wheelchair, saying, "My church is on TBN, and I'm a pastor. This is why I brought you. My mother-in-law has surgery Monday morning." I prayed for the woman, and later I was taken to a loft to sleep. The next morning, I awoke to the smell of bacon and eggs—and the sound of a knock. It was the mother-in-law—**walking.** She hadn't walked in three years!

That day, we saw eighty people baptized, tumors fell off, and deaf ears were unstopped. God moved with power.

But then came the test. The pastor took me to his car lot, told me to pick any car I wanted. I had just started a small church in the hood—about a hundred members, all on welfare. I walked past the Cadillacs, the Bentleys, and pointed right at the Rolls-Royce. I drove that Rolls straight into the hood.

By the next service, every member had quit. I had faith for the Rolls—but no wisdom for the moment. I was out of harmony with my assignment. You must never live above the crowd you are called to serve. The blessing is not for display—it's for development. I should've used that blessing to lift the people, not leave them.

Faith without wisdom breaks harmony. The Word says,

> *Let no one seek his own, but each one the other's well-being.*
>
> 1 Corinthians 10:24

Your individual victory should lead to the band's collective triumph. When you walk in unity—faith joined with wisdom—you not only secure your deliverance, you secure the freedom of everyone around you.

The Locust's Declaration of Unity

Father, thank You for the wisdom of the Locust. Today I declare that I will no longer walk in isolation, pride, or self-interest. I submit to the Law of Harmony and align myself with the sound of Heaven and the body of Christ.

Remove from me every spirit of jealousy, competition, and division. Teach me how to walk in one accord, so Your power can flow freely through my life and through my circle.

Help me discern the right connections and release the wrong ones. Give me the courage to walk away from what breaks my rhythm and the wisdom to recognize who belongs in my next season.

Father, make me a part of the band that moves with power, unity, and clarity of purpose. Together we rise, together we move, and together we win.

In Jesus' name—Amen.

Part Two:

Deliverance through Fire

Feed the Flame, Guard the Oil, and Let Every Stronghold Fall—Your Deliverance Is Here!

Chapter 4

The Anointing That Destroys the Yoke

The **Ant** is small, but wise. It gathers while others rest, preparing for what's ahead.

The **Cony** hides in the rock, protected from the enemy.

The **Locust** moves in unity, finding strength in numbers.

Each one reveals a spiritual principle—*how to move, how to build, how to endure.*

But now we come to the **Spider**, the fourth small thing—*silent, strategic, and patient.* She doesn't rely on size or strength. Her power lies in **access**. She finds her way into the palace, building in secret places. And just like her, there are spiritual spiders that creep into the sacred spaces of your life—*your heart, your home, your ministry*—feeding off what has been left uncovered.

Before we can **prevent** the Spider from taking hold, we must first understand what **attracts her**. The Spider is drawn to **decay**—to the stench of **spoiled oil** and stale atmospheres. When the oil of the **anointing** is left uncovered—when **consecration fades** and the **fire burns low**—the scent changes. What once carried the fragrance of worship now carries the **smell of neglect**.

Let me tell you a story. When I was pastoring in Columbus, Ohio, the building needed fixing. There was a hole in the roof that we kept saying we'd get to soon. Delay after delay. Excuse after excuse. We were busy doing ministry, preaching, praying—but not fixing what was broken.

I had been away from the church for three days. When I walked into my office, I was **shocked**. There were **thousands of dead flies everywhere**. The smell was **unbearable**, and nearly **$20,000 worth of furniture** had been ruined.

It was then that we finally looked at the roof and discovered the source: a dead squirrel, half-eaten and alive with maggots, the air above it buzzing with flies. The squirrel was **not the real problem**—the hole in the roof was. What had been left **unaddressed** allowed decay to enter.

In that moment, the Holy Ghost spoke, "Son, this is what happens when you delay fixing what's broken."

When you ignore the holes in your ministry—the cracks in your character, the compromises in your spirit—you invite death to move in. And death always draws flies. Flies draw spiders. What you refuse to **repair** will rot. What you leave open, the **enemy will occupy**. Decay multiplies fast. Just three days of neglect, and the **anointing begins to spoil**. *You cannot patch spiritual decay with busy work or borrowed fire.* **Fix the hole! Fix your ministry! Fix your heart! Fix your discipline!**

The Oil and Its Flow

Unchecked neglect doesn't just leave a mess; it corrupts your **spiritual flow.** *Your oil is your anointing—the sacred presence and empowerment of God in your life.* It is **holy**. It is **weighty**. It is **costly**. But just as natural oil can become **contaminated**, so can your anointing when small compromises and **unaddressed sins** are left unchecked.

This contamination doesn't stay hidden. Scripture warns,

> *Dead flies cause the ointment of the apothecary to send forth a stinking savour*
>
> Ecclesiastes 10:1

King Solomon noted, *"It stinketh."* What once drew God's presence now **repels Him**.

And this is why **your anointing affects everything around you.** That oil flows into your **testimony, your influence, and the spiritual atmosphere of your home and ministry.** *What you allow to spoil in private will ripple outward into public impact; everything connected to you is affected.*

Some of us are still anointed, but our oil has been sitting **uncovered**. The **flies** of offense, gossip, jealousy, and distraction have landed in it. And the scent of those dead flies is what attracts the **Spider**. The Spider doesn't come without a reason—it is drawn to **decay**, to the stench of **spoiled oil.** *Where there is spiritual rot, there will always be a web.*

You can't keep sweeping cobwebs and think you've solved the problem. The **cobwebs** are only evidence—the stinking savor that draws the **Spider**. Until you deal with the **source**, the Spider will keep coming back. You can't pray your way out of an atmosphere you refuse to **change**.

Restoring the Fire and Preventing the Spider

To prevent the Spider from taking hold, *we must restore the fire,* because the *intensity of the flame determines the strength of the fragrance,* and the *strength of the fragrance reveals the quality of the anointing.* When the fire burns **bright**, the oil stays **pure**. When the flame dies down, the oil grows **stale**—and a stale anointing loses its **power**.

That is why the **High Priest** carried a sacred responsibility: to keep the **Menorah**—the golden candlestick—burning with *fresh fire and fresh oil.* In the Old Testament, the Menorah represented the very presence of God in the sanctuary. Crafted of **pure gold**, it stood as a symbol of **divine perfection**—seven arms for the **seven Spirits of God.** At the top of each arm burned a **wick**, representing **Jesus, the Light of the World.** The oil flowing through the base symbolized the **Holy Ghost**, rich with fragrance, because *true anointing always carries the scent of praise and worship.*

Moses captures the sacred duty of the priest:

And Aaron shall burn thereon sweet incense every morning: when he dresseth the lamps, he shall burn incense upon it. And when Aaron lighteth the lamps at even, he shall burn incense upon it, a perpetual incense before the LORD throughout your generations.

Exodus 30:7–8

The passage reminds us that maintaining the fire was **not optional**—it was **perpetual**, a continual act of consecration and devotion.

The High Priest had one command: *keep the fire burning and the oil fresh.* He could not use **strange fire**—borrowed inspiration from other altars, voices, or sources. The flame had to be **authentic**, born out of **personal sacrifice**, kindled by a heart laid **prostrate before God**. True fire does not come from imitation; it comes from **intimacy**.

True fire does not come from imitation; **it comes from intimacy**. It is the product of communion, not performance. The altar burned continually, not because of duty, but because of devotion.

> *Behold, thou art fair, my beloved, yea, pleasant: also our bed is green.*
> *Song of Solomon 1:16*

A **green bed** symbolizes **life and fruitfulness**—a love that produces growth rather than stagnation. In the same way, our relationship with God should be **alive, fertile, and continually producing fruit**. Love with God should never be sterile; it should overflow with evidence of His life in us.

> *Abide in me, and I in you. As the branch cannot bear fruit of itself, except it abide in the vine; no more can ye, except ye abide in me... He that abideth in me, and I in him, the same bringeth forth much fruit.*
> *John 15:4–5*

Intimacy with God is not emotional hype—it is a sustained connection. When you dwell in Him and He dwells in you, **love produces fruit.** Passion becomes purpose. Fire becomes fragrance. What begins as worship in private turns into **power in public.**

Love is what keeps the flame burning hot.
Love is the oil that never runs out.
Love is the secret fire of the inner court.

If the priest let the flame die, darkness filled the temple. In the same way, when intimacy fades, the light of revelation dims. But when love burns, the oil flows, and **the presence of God becomes tangible** once again.

Keep the fire burning. Keep the oil fresh. Let your love for Him stay green and alive.

In the same way, today's pastor carries that charge—to keep the **candlestick lit and the flame high.** When the flame burns **hot**, the oil **heats up.** That heat saturates everything around it, making the anointing **tangible and alive.** *But if the fire grows dim, flies—symbols of* ***corruption, compromise, and distraction****—slip past the flame into the oil, and the anointing begins to* ***stink****.*

Not only will spoiled oil affect you personally, but it also spreads beyond your reach. Consider the **Santa Barbara oil spill** about ten years ago. A tanker's hull was **busted**, and oil leaked into the ocean. Some of it could be contained, but most spread far beyond anyone's immediate control, damaging **ecosystems** and affecting **lives across the coast.** *Your spiritual oil works the same way—what starts as private neglect can impact things you never intended and cannot control.* **Contaminated oil spreads into areas far beyond your reach,** affecting everything and everyone connected to your sphere of influence.

Lukewarmness

God *will not release fresh anointing* until the **holes** of hurt, compromise, or distraction that allow contamination to persist are addressed. Sometimes, **people, patterns, or entire seasons** must be set aside to restore **purity.** As we have already see, **your circle creates your cycles.** *Your circle can either protect or poison your flow.*

The **Laodicean church** illustrates this principle. Their waters—**stolen from the abundant supply of Philadelphia**—became **lukewarm** by the time they reached Laodicea. Lukewarm waters were **infected with parasites,** causing **stillborn births and blindness. Hierapolis** had **therapeutic hot springs,** medicinal and healing. **Colossae** had **cold mountain water,** refreshing and life-giving. By the time the aqueducts carried Hierapolis and Colossae's stolen water to Laodicea, it was neither hot nor cold—it was **lukewarm,** and **vulnerable to corruption.**

Spiritually, this shows the danger when **fire burns low in your heart**. Parasites—the **enemy, distractions, compromise**—thrive in lukewarmness.

Too hot, they die. Too cold, they die. But lukewarmness allows **spiritual contamination** to grow. God said He would **spue lukewarm churches out of His mouth** because the contamination is **intolerable**. When the **anointing loses its heat**, it stops being **life-giving**; it becomes **dangerous**.

John reminds us in the final book:

> *I know thy works, that thou art neither cold nor hot: I would thou wert cold or hot. So then because thou art lukewarm, and neither cold nor hot, I will spue thee out of my mouth. I counsel thee to buy of me gold tried in the fire, that thou mayest be rich...*
>
> Revelation 3:14–22

Turn up the heat in your **prayer, devotion, and consecration**, so that **lukewarmness does not infect your anointing**.

Living in the Fire

Your deliverance is not about **sweeping cobwebs**—it is about living **too hot for spiders to abide**. When your fire burns bright, your oil stays **pure**, and the atmosphere around you becomes **inhospitable to the enemy**. The same anointing that protects your **heart and ministry** also carries the **power to break every yoke** and remove every **burden** in your life.

> *And it shall come to pass in that day, that his burden shall be taken away from off thy shoulder, and his yoke from off thy neck, and the yoke shall be destroyed because of the anointing.*
>
> Isaiah 10:27

You are **free**. You may have thrown in the towel, but God **threw it back**. You may have gotten yourself into a **mess**, but God will **get you out**. The anointing is here to **prevent the spider** and **destroy the yoke**.

Ask yourself: Where has the fire in your life **burned low**? Have you tolerated **small flies**—habits, thoughts, or attitudes—that have begun to **spoil your oil**? Ask the Holy Spirit to reveal any **areas where your spiritual roof is weak**. Some holes may seem small, but they serve as **entry points for decay**. Restore the **fire** through prayer and worship, and the **fragrance of your anointing** will shift—the atmosphere around you will **come alive**.

Prayer of Fresh Oil

*Father, I thank You for the **oil** that destroys the **yoke**. I ask You to burn away every **dead thing** in me—every old habit, every compromise, every spiritual hole I've ignored. Teach me to protect what You have poured into my life. Turn up the **fire** again, Lord. Make my heart the **altar** where **fresh oil flows**.*

*I refuse to live with **dead flies**. I refuse to let my **anointing spoil**. Cleanse me, purify me, and restore the **fragrance** of Your presence. If there are people, patterns, or wounds that contaminate my flow, give me the courage to separate and the humility to heal.*

*Let the **fire of the Holy Ghost** burn hot in my life until every **distraction, every weight, and every spider** is prevented from taking hold. Keep me **consecrated**—set apart and refined. Protect my **oil**, preserve my **purity**, and guard my **spirit** from contamination.*

*Father, keep my **oil pure**, keep my **fire high**, and keep my **spirit fresh**.*

In Jesus' name, Amen.

Chapter 5

The Webs:

The Three Traps of Deception

We have established that the **anointing is the atmosphere that prevents the Spider**. But when the enemy sees a prepared believer, he changes tactics, weaving a net designed to trap you in predictable, repeating cycles.

The Spider is all about **access and execution**. His weapon is the net—the spiritual web—and it is designed to trap you in the old temptations you keep falling for, the debt you cannot shake, the anger you cannot surrender. As Prince Agur said, the spider

taketh hold with her hands, and is in king's palaces
Proverbs 30:28

It is a multi-handed attack. If he can't get you, he will attack your children. If he cannot entangle your finances, he seeks to create anarchy in your home—growth one week, setback the next.

Do not be deceived: sometimes the people closest to you become the instruments of the enemy. He knows your routines. He knows the **luggage you left on the ground** when you thought you had crucified the flesh. If you still harbor lust for sin, the Spider has already set the trap.

You must **identify the trap**. There are **three specific webs** designed to catch you.

The first trap is the **Funnel Web**—the trap of **Hypocrisy**. This web is spun in the **corners of your spiritual life**. It represents the **spirit of the false prophet** in your circle. They won't shout, dance, or praise God openly. But after service, they corner you with a "word from God," appearing spiritual while **subtly shaking the collar with venom**. This web looks like a blessing, but is often a disguised curse.

These kinds of webs **seduce people into believing a form of truth**. They **speak truth without transformation**, offering insight without intimacy. Their words sound holy, but they lack the weight of heaven. They are good for **highlighting your past**, but **they cannot speak into your future** because they have not stood in the presence of the God who writes it.

The Funnel Web looks narrow at the top—appearing focused and pure—but its purpose is to **draw you downward**. Like a whisper that becomes a storm, their flattery initially feels affirming but slowly erodes conviction. The more you listen, the more you drift—away from discernment, away from accountability, and deeper into deception.

Paul warned of these voices when he wrote,

> *Having a form of godliness, but denying the power thereof"*
>
> *2 Timothy 3:5*

These are people who can **speak in tongues but not in truth**, who can preach about deliverance but live in bondage. They sound anointed but lack authority.

Before long, you find yourself imitating their rhythm—**using spiritual language without spiritual life**, performing rather than dwelling. You shout in church, but go home unchanged. You begin to confuse noise for power and emotion for presence. That's how the Funnel Web traps its prey—not through open sin, but through subtle imitation of the sacred.

The second trap is the **Sticky Web**—the trap of **Shame**. This is the web that catches you with memories, habits, and cycles you thought were dead. You don't fall into it once; you *return* to it—pulled back by guilt, fear, and unfinished repentance. It's the addiction that keeps calling your name, the debt that keeps resurfacing, the relationship you know isn't good for you but still feels familiar.

The more you struggle to free yourself, the tighter it holds. Shame is the adhesive that binds the soul to its yesterday. The enemy doesn't have to invent new traps when old ones still work—he adds fresh reminders of failure to make you stop believing in freedom. That's why Scripture warns,

> *As a dog returneth to his vomit, so a fool returneth to his folly*
>
> Proverbs 26:11

This web doesn't just trap your actions—it **poisons your identity**. You begin to see yourself through the lens of what happened, not what God said. You start believing that forgiveness applies to others but not to you. It tells you to stay quiet in worship because you "don't deserve to lift your hands." It convinces you that your mistakes are permanent, your calling has been revoked, and your destiny has been forfeited.

But hear this clearly: **shame is not conviction**. Conviction points you forward; shame keeps you stuck. Conviction says, "Come out." Shame whispers, "Stay hidden." And the more you hide, the more the web tightens.

This is why the enemy loves the Sticky Web—it keeps you living in loops. You shout about deliverance but go home to the same chains. You quote Scripture but secretly believe it doesn't apply to you. That's how shame disguises itself as humility: you think you're being honest, but you're actually being held hostage.

Here is a prophecy from God for you:

> *For your shame I will give you double; for confusion they shall rejoice in their portion: therefore in their land they shall possess the double: everlasting joy shall be unto them*
>
> Isaiah 61:7

God is telling you that the cycles that held you down, the shame that weighed on your soul, the regrets that haunted your nights—they are not the end of your story. Every chain is a seed for a double blessing. Every failure is a pathway to greater honor. Every shame-filled memory is a shadow that will be eclipsed by everlasting joy.

The Psalmist declared,

> *He lifted me out of the miry clay, and set my feet upon a rock*
>
> Psalm 40:2

That means **you were not designed to stay stuck**. The same hands that formed you are strong enough to free you. The Sticky Web may cling to your life, but God's promise is stronger: your shame will be replaced with double honor, your past will produce fruit, and the cycles that held you captive will be broken.

Stand up. Lift your hands. Step into the portion God has prepared for you—where shame is swallowed, confusion turned to clarity, and everlasting joy becomes your inheritance.

FLAT WEB

The third trap is the **Flat Web**—the trap of **Complacency**. This one is the most dangerous because it doesn't look like a trap at all. It lies beneath what's comfortable, hidden under the furniture of routine, waiting for stillness to settle. You don't stumble into this web; you grow into it slowly, through comfort that replaces hunger and success that replaces pursuit.

The Flat Web forms when you start confusing stability with surrender. **You've stopped running to sin—but you've also stopped running to God.** You've plateaued spiritually. You no longer expect more, no longer pray with fire, no longer move with urgency. The danger isn't rebellion—it's resignation.

This web thrives in **unmoved furniture**—areas of your life you refuse to shift. That secret habit you call "manageable." That bitterness you keep under the rug. That relationship, you know, isn't aligned but feels too comfortable to confront. Beneath every unmoved thing is a web quietly collecting dust and death.

Proverbs warns,

> *Yet a little sleep, a little slumber, a little folding of the hands to sleep: So shall thy poverty come as one that travelleth*
>
> *Proverbs 24:33–34*

Spiritual poverty begins when motion stops. The longer you stay still, the more your discernment dulls, and before long, you can no longer tell the difference between peace and paralysis.

The Flat Web lulls believers into thinking, "I'm fine." But fine is not fruitful. Fine is not fiery. Fine is the slow fade from purpose to passivity. This is why Revelation warns,

> *Because thou art lukewarm, and neither cold nor hot, I will spue thee out of my mouth*
>
> *Revelation 3:16*

Lukewarmness is not just a temperature—it's a condition of surrender without pursuit, faith without flame.

And here lies the great deception: the enemy doesn't have to make you sin—he just has to make you *settle*. The moment you stop pressing, the web begins forming beneath your feet.

Once you identify the type of web, you can locate the Spider. You are no longer fighting the entanglement—you are preparing to **destroy the source.**

But there's something deeper here. **These three webs don't just symbolize traps; they also reveal witchcraft in the pews.** The same spirit that spins deception in your private life often creeps into public worship. The same Spider that whispers in your ear on Monday shows up dressed in white on Sunday.

Let me explain. I have preached in third-world countries—Jamaica, Barbados, Ghana, Trinidad, and Montreal, Quebec, Canada—and I have noticed a familiar trend. When the Spirit gets high and the fire burns, **dancing breaks out.** But not all dances are in the Spirit. Some dances appear to be **vibrations designed to free the trapped**, but they are often **seductions disguised as freedom**.

These vibrations **signal the Spider** that someone is stuck in a web, ready to be devoured. I see this trend in some American churches today. Some dances are **not holy dancing**. They are **traps for single women and men alike**, designed to lure them into the Spider's snare.

Contrast this with **David**, who danced before the Ark of the Covenant (2 Samuel 6). He danced **out of submission, not seduction**. The Spirit fueled his dance. One of his wives, Michal, misinterpreted the dance and spoke against it, and a curse fell on her womb. We must **discern between true worshippers and impersonators**. John teaches,

> *God is a Spirit: and they that worship him must worship him in spirit and in truth.*
>
> *John 4:24*

The enemy uses the **webs of deception**—temptation, manipulation, pride, seduction—to trap believers. Jesus Himself faced every possible web. In Matthew 4, the devil spun webs of temptation, offering kingdoms, wealth, and power. He twisted scripture, offered shortcuts, and set layers of deception. But **Jesus remained in the will of the Father**. He said, **"It is written"** with every attempt. He did not fall into the web because He stayed in God's will. Staying in God's will keeps you **out of the Spider's trap**.

Paul reminds us,

> *Put on the whole armor of God, that ye may be able to stand against the wiles of the devil. For we wrestle not against flesh and blood, but against principalities, against powers, against the rulers of the darkness of this world, against spiritual wickedness in high places.*
>
> Ephesians 6:11-12

Every web, every trap, every layer of temptation—financial, relational, sexual, or spiritual—is **designed to distract, deceive, and delay you.** But the same anointing that destroyed the Spider in your life can also **expose every hidden web**, reveal the root of deception, and destroy the enemy's access.

You must **maintain intimacy with God, guard your spiritual roof**, and **keep the fire burning**. Crucify the flesh (Galatians 5:24). Lay down the old habits of the flesh, the patterns of doubt, worry, and negativity. Do not dance in imitation; do not worship with false vibration. **Let the Holy Spirit lead** your worship, your ministry, and your battle.

When the webs are exposed, when the fire is hot, and the oil flows pure, the Spider **loses access**. The habits, the routines, the secret sins—everything the Spider relied on—is destroyed in the presence of God. You are free to move forward in **power, purpose, and authority**, untouched by the nets that once held you.

Prayer of Deliverance from the Webs

*Father, I thank You for revealing the Spider's traps in my life. Today, I choose to **identify every web of deception** and expose every hidden snare. I break the Funnel Web of hypocrisy, the Sticky Web of shame, and the Flat Web of complacency. I declare that **no entanglement of the enemy** will hold me, my family, or my ministry.*

*Lord, I refuse to be caught in the old cycles of temptation, debt, anger, or compromise. **I crucify the flesh** with its affections and lusts. I lay down doubt, worry, negativity, and every lingering habit that gives the enemy access. I will **stay in Your will**, and in Your will I will remain untouched by the Spider.*

*Restore my fire, Father. Let my worship be **spirit-led**, my ministry Spirit-filled, and my heart fully surrendered. Let the fragrance of Your presence flow through me, making every net and trap powerless. I receive the **anointing to expose deception and destroy the enemy's access** in every area of my life.*

*Father, let every layer of temptation be revealed, every snare broken, and every web consumed in the fire of Your Spirit. I will move forward **free, bold, and victorious**, walking in discernment, power, and authority.*

*In Jesus' name—**Amen**.*

Chapter 6

The Spiders:

Exposing Demonic Schemes

The spider taketh hold with her hands, and is in kings' palaces.

Proverbs 30:28

We have identified the nets—the effects. Now we must confront the spiders—the root cause. These are the specific demonic spirits that must be **exposed, conquered, and cast out of your palace once and for all.**

Before you can slay anything, you have to **wake up your own spirit.** Stop accepting the dead spiritual atmosphere around you. You cannot afford to be numb while the glory is falling. **The dead flies have to be removed.** Shake yourself. Speak life into your own bones.

> *But they that wait upon the Lord shall renew their strength; they shall mount up with wings as eagles; they shall run, and not be weary; and they shall walk, and not faint.*
>
> *Isaiah 40:31*

The Loxosceles: Digging for Destruction

The first spider we encounter is the Loxosceles Spider, also known as the ditch-digger. This spider digs spiritual pits, waiting for you to stumble into despair and never climb out. It whispers, *"You'll never recover,"* every time you fall. Its goal is to bury you alive in shame, regret, and hopelessness.

But **God never leaves His people in the ditch.** Throughout Scripture, He turns pits into platforms and prisons into pulpits. **Paul and Silas** were locked in a cell, beaten and bound, but at midnight, they began to pray and sing praises to God. **And suddenly,** the earth shook, the doors flew open, and every chain fell loose. **The same dungeon that was meant to silence them became the place where their deliverance thundered.**

Daniel was thrown into a lion's den, but the mouths of the lions were shut. When morning came, the same men who dug his ditch were cast into it themselves.

LOXOSCELES
SPIDER

Shadrach, Meshach, and Abednego were thrown into the fire—but before they ever entered, the soldiers who carried them were consumed by the very flames they meant for God's servants. What a divine reversal! **The fire that was meant to destroy them became the furnace of their testimony.** Not only did they survive the flames, **but the Fourth Man—Jesus Himself—stepped into the fire with them.**

When God walks with you in the heat, what was designed to burn you will only refine you. Their bonds were burned, but their bodies were untouched. Their faith became fireproof. **The same fire that killed their captors became the place where God revealed His glory.**

And **Joseph,** betrayed by his own brothers, was thrown into a pit. But God raised him up from the dungeon to the palace, and in the end, Joseph declared,

> *You meant it for evil, but God meant it for good.*
> *Genesis 50:20*

The same pit that was meant to end him became the platform that saved his family and preserved a nation.

The Loxosceles Spider's assignment is discouragement and self-pity. Its venom convinces you to stay down, to sit in sorrow instead of standing in strength. But when **praise rises,** ditches become **altars of victory.**

Sing unto the Lord, O ye saints of his, and give thanks at the remembrance of his holiness."

Psalm 30:4

Praise is the ladder that lifts you out. The moment you worship, walls tremble, and webs break. What the enemy dug for your death becomes the very ground where your miracle manifests.

I will not die in depression; I will dance over it. I will not drown in despair; I will step on it as a bridge into destiny. **Every ditch designed for my destruction will become evidence of my deliverance.**

What the enemy meant for evil, God has turned for good—and for the enemy's own demise.

Help me kill this spider.

. . .

Now that the ditch-digger has been crushed, the next web to unravel is deception.

The Wolf Spider: Pulpit Predator

The **Wolf Spider**, the **false prophet**, hunts not in darkness but in daylight—camouflaged in collars, robes, fine suits, and pulpits. It preaches on Sunday, but its appetite is flesh, not faith. *It moves from church to church,*

WOLF
SPIDER

preying on the vulnerable—feeding not on faith but on flesh. It manipulates through flattery, seduces through "words from the Lord," and feeds on attention, money, and control. Its prophecies sound accurate but are barren of fruit, for they are not birthed in God's presence but rehearsed through deceit.

> *But there were false prophets also among the people… and many shall follow their pernicious ways.*
> 2 Peter 2:1–2

> *For such are false apostles, deceitful workers, transforming themselves into the apostles of Christ.*
> 2 Corinthians 11:13

These spiders are **active hunters**, skilled in camouflage and spiritual mimicry. They study churches from afar—scrolling through social media, gathering details, learning faces—then arrive, appearing prophetic, calling names they found online as if heaven whispered them. **But they are mirages and clouds without water.**

They wear many colors and collars, appearing righteous but living ruthlessly. **They speak truth without transformation, prophecy without power, and revelation without repentance.** They are good at recalling the past, but they cannot speak into your future because they are not connected to the Source.

The Wolf Spider's goal is destruction through seduction. **It creeps into families, weaving webs around**

leaders and their households. It whispers comfort while plotting corruption. It sizes you up like a serpent, telling you what you want to hear until rebellion turns to perversion and perversion births destruction for their prey. This spirit doesn't want deliverance—it wants destruction through domination. It isolates, manipulates, and feeds on the people of God.

But when light hits camouflage, the hunter is revealed.

After you read this, every false prophet, every manipulative spirit, every wolf hiding in sheep's clothing will be exposed by the fire of discernment. **That spirit that tried to devour your home, your peace, and your children is being dismantled right now in the name of Jesus.** God is uncovering hidden agendas and driving out deception.

The Wolf Spider dies when truth is spoken.

Once discernment awakens, deception has nowhere left to hide. You have authority. You have vision. You have the blood of Jesus as your covering. No false voice can speak over your life again.

Help me kill this spider.

...

Now that **deception has been exposed**, we turn to a spider that doesn't hunt by sight or sound—but by **contact**. This one doesn't need to deceive you; it only needs to **touch you.**

It moves through circles, relationships, and even ministry lines, transferring its venom from vessel to vessel.

The Hopping Spider: Spirit of Contamination

This is the **Hopping Spider**—the spirit of **transference and contamination**. When deceit is unmasked, contamination comes crawling. This next spider doesn't spin lies—it transfers poison. The Hopping Spider leaps from vessel to vessel, from hand to hand, carrying unholy influence wherever there is an open door.

The **Hopping Spider** doesn't weave a stationary web; it moves.

It leaps from host to host, spreading defilement through **improper contact**, **careless laying on of hands**, and **unholy connections**.

It operates in the shadows of fellowship—through hugs, handshakes, and emotional ties that seem harmless but carry hidden infection.

> *Lay hands suddenly on no man, neither be partaker of other men's sins: keep thyself pure.*
>
> 1 Timothy 5:22

HOPPING
SPIDER

This spider thrives where **discernment is absent** and **souls are desperate for affirmation**. It disguises contamination as connection. But what feels like fellowship is sometimes **a spiritual exchange**, a transfer of energy, emotion, and influence.

The Hopping Spider loves worship settings where **hands are lifted but hearts are unguarded**. It searches for openings in **unhealed souls**—those hungry for touch but not yet whole.

That's why we must draw **bloodlines**, not walls. The **blood of Jesus** is our barrier—it does not isolate, but it insulates.

Just as in Egypt, when the plague passed over every door marked with blood, so too must the saints mark their **homes, hands, and hearts** with the covenant covering.

No spirit shall hop from pew to pew, post to post, hand to hand.

The **bloodline** is drawn.

Every **unauthorized transference** is canceled. Every **unholy exchange** is reversed. Every **contaminated impartation** is broken in Jesus' name.

You are **anointed, not infected**.

Your touch will **heal, not transfer harm**.

Your embrace will **impart peace, not poison.**

Help me kill this spider.

. . .

After the Hopping Spider's poison is exposed, another spirit slithers in—glittering with promise but hollow at its core. The Hati Hati Spider spins praise that depends on prosperity. It thrives where worship is weighed by wallets and faith fades with fortune.

The Hati Hati: The Curse of Conditional Praise

The Hati Hati Spider represents the **Prosperity Spirit** that dances only when the coffers are full. Its silk glistens with gold but carries no glory. It is attractive, but empty; dazzling, but deceptive. This spider thrives in atmospheres where praise is contingent upon possessions and worship is dictated by wealth.

Its web glimmers in the light of success, but cannot withstand the wind of testing. When the car breaks down or the account runs low, this spirit begins to whisper, "Where is your God now?" Its venom infects faith with conditional worship—praise that exists only in comfort. Yet the Word of God declares:

HATI HATI
SPIDER

> *"Though the fig tree shall not blossom, neither shall fruit be in the vines... yet I will rejoice in the Lord, I will joy in the God of my salvation."*
>
> Habakkuk 3:17–18

> *Let your light so shine before men, that they may see your good works, and glorify your Father which is in heaven.*
>
> Matthew 5:16

Worship in famine burns the Hati Hati spider.

We declare:
I praise Him in plenty and in lack. My worship is not for sale. My devotion is not affected by the balance in my account.

But this spider has another face—the **Fair-Weather Christian.** The Hati Hati Spirit survives only in controlled environments, thriving where comfort is king. Its favorite word is *control*—and that reveals its true ancestry. Control is the language of **Jezebel**.

The Hati Hati Spirit, like Jezebel, is not defined by gender but by domination. It seeks to control money, manipulate influence, and consume resources until nothing remains but dependence and despair. Jezebel ruled her husband, devoured the prophets, and even manipulated Israel's economy through possession of land and territory.

Remember Ahab and **Naboth's vineyard.** Ahab wanted what was not his, and when Naboth refused to sell,

Jezebel schemed, lied, and murdered to seize it. That was not just greed—it was a form of **territorial warfare.**

This same territorial spirit is embodied in the Hati Hati Spider. It wants your vineyard—your God-given inheritance, your place of provision, your ministry, your peace. It will use manipulation, flattery, or financial strain to make you surrender what belongs to God.

But I declare: **My vineyard is not for sale.** My worship, my purpose, my territory—none of it belongs to the enemy.

When I praise in famine, the Hati Hati Spider loses its hold. When I give even in lack, the gold web collapses under the weight of true glory. For the Kingdom's economy does not run on coins but on **covenant.**

I am not controlled by currency—I am covered by Christ.

Help me kill this spider.

...

Once shallow praise is silenced, hypocrisy steps forward. The Two-Faced Spider wears masks of devotion but weaves threads of deceit. It smiles in the sanctuary and schemes in the shadows, speaking blessing in public while spreading poison in private.

The Two-Faced Spider: Weaving the Web of Deceit and Contamination

The Two-Faced Spider may not look the most dangerous—it doesn't strike with the immediate fear of the Black Widow or the boldness of the Tarantula—but make no mistake, it is far more lethal. This spider is dangerous because it is **two-faced**. It smiles while it schemes. It plays with you for days, eats with you, prays with you, worships beside you, and waits until it gathers just enough of your trust—then it bites.

This spider represents people who shout, worship, and pray right next to you, not because they love God, but because they are studying you. They gather your pain, your secrets, and your patterns—not to heal, but to harm. They will embrace you in public and betray you in private.

The spider doesn't just want to trap you; he wants to **connect with you**—to weave you into a covenant that doesn't belong to you. This is why I don't sit at every table or eat with just anyone. In Hebrew tradition, to break bread is a sacred act. It means *covenant*. The one you eat with becomes part of your spiritual household.

TWO FACE
SPIDER

There was a woman who knew this truth. She came with her alabaster box, broke it open, and poured out what others called waste. While they whispered about her past, Jesus received her worship. She washed His feet with her tears and dried them with her hair—not for show, but for surrender. That moment was not about perfume—it was about **preparation.** *She discerned His purpose before they discerned His presence.* She anointed His walk before the world knew that the cross called His name.

Even here, the spider lurked—jealousy, judgment, and distraction tried to contaminate the altar. But discernment shields the holy. She refused the spider's bait, recognizing that where her worship fell determined what would be carried forward.

Because when you know what's holy, **you handle it differently.** You don't sit at every table. You don't walk in every circle. *You guard your oil, and you protect your feet—*because **where you walk determines what you carry.**

When God told Moses,

> *Take off your shoes, for the place where you stand is holy ground*
>
> *Exodus 3:5*

It wasn't only about reverence—it was about removing the dirt of his past before stepping into purpose. God didn't want the dust of Egypt tracking into His glory. **You can't make it to Canaan with Egypt on your mind.**

You can't enter the promise carrying old ways, old habits, and old traditions. The spider's purpose is to remind you of Egypt—to keep you circling in the wilderness of your past, never stepping into the land of promise.

God commanded in *Numbers 33:52*:

> *Then ye shall drive out all the inhabitants of the land from before you, and destroy all their pictures, and destroy all their molten images, and quite pluck down all their high places.*

You must **drive out** every image, every idol, every high place that represents your old self. You cannot conquer Canaan while still entertaining Egypt. You must evict the memories, destroy the idols, and silence the voices that keep calling you back to the place God delivered you from.

Because hear me—the spider thrives in the soil of your past. If you don't clean the dirt off your feet, he'll spin a web right where your deliverance should be.

Even the smallest spider dares to dwell in royal chambers. So too, demons seek to build webs in the hearts of God's chosen—silently spinning fear, pride, lust, and deception in places meant for glory. Before the palace can host His presence, the invaders must be exposed.

You cannot continue walking with unclean people who keep you tethered to the dirt of your past. Some are not companions—they are contaminants. You cannot dine with betrayal and expect deliverance.

Help me kill this spider.

...

Deception confronted, double-mindedness destroyed—yet beneath the surface waits another hunter. The Trap-Door Spider hides in unseen holes, devouring the fruit of your labor and draining the oil of your anointing. It is the silent devourer of increase.

The Trap-Door Spider: Silent Devourer of Harvest and Anointing

The Trap-Door Spider hides under opportunity, waiting to swallow your harvest. You don't see it until your resources start disappearing—until you're wondering how you tithe, how you give, and still seem to come up short. Its presence manifests in cycles of debt, lack, and frustration—a spiritual and financial drought that never seems to end.

> *Bring ye all the tithes into the storehouse… and prove me now herewith, saith the Lord of hosts, if I will not open you the windows of heaven, and pour you out a blessing, that there shall not be room enough to receive it.*
> *Malachi 3:10*

TRAP DOOR
SPIDER

Your **tithe belongs to God**—it's holy, it's His, and returning it to Him positions you under divine protection. But **the seed** is different. The seed is what you give after you've tithed—it's the overflow of faith and obedience.

The enemy knows the **laws of harvest**—he understands that:

> *whatsoever a man soweth, that shall he also reap*
> *Galatians 6:7*

so he does everything he can to keep you from planting.

He whispers, "You can't afford to give right now." He tempts you to give God your leftover change instead of your best. He convinces you to hold your seed so tightly that it never leaves your hand—and therefore never enters your future.

But when you sow—**name your seed.** Don't just drop it in the ground; *speak over it.* Declare what you want that seed to do in the earth and in your life. You can name your seed *healing, debt cancellation, family salvation, unity in the church, business breakthrough,* or *new dimensions.*

> *Death and life are in the power of the tongue: and they that love it shall eat the fruit thereof.*
> *Proverbs 18:21*

Every time you sow, you are **speaking life** into the soil of your future. You are prophesying your harvest before you ever see it.

When **Hannah** cried out in bitterness of soul and vowed a vow before the Lord (1 Samuel 1:11), she *named her seed*. Her offering wasn't just a sacrifice—it was *Samuel,* the son she longed for and promised to dedicate to God. She spoke her seed's assignment before it ever took root, and Heaven moved.

So when you sow, open your mouth and declare:

This seed is for my healing.
This seed is for the deliverance of my children.
This seed is for unity in my home.
This seed will break the curse of debt in my life.

Your seed is not just money—it's **a prophetic act.** Your declaration solidifies that the enemy will not eat your harvest. When you tithe, sow, and decree God's Word over your seed, **the trapdoor slams shut on the devourer.**

You've been faithful; your harvest belongs to God. The spider cannot touch what is covered by obedience. The Lord Himself has promised: *"I will rebuke the devourer for your sakes."* The trap is broken, the curse is reversed, and your seed is about to speak.

But there's more—because **a seed will stop a cycle.**

Just like a seed in a woman stops her cycle and produces life in nine months, I prophesy that within *nine months* your harvest will begin to manifest.

Look at **Isaac** in Genesis 26:18–25.

> *And Isaac digged again the wells of water, which they had digged in the days of Abraham his father; for the Philistines had stopped them after the death of Abraham: and he called their names after the names by which his father had called them.*

In the valley of **Gerar**, Isaac sowed seed in the land—and *in that same year,* he reaped a **hundredfold return.** But his blessing didn't come without battle.

The **first well** he dug struck water, but that night the Philistines filled it with dirt. Isaac called it **Esek,** meaning *contention*. That's the spider's job—to plug your wells, to block your flow, to choke the life out of your abundance.

Isaac didn't stop there. He dug **another well** and named it **Sitnah,** which means *strife and opposition*. Again, the enemy tried to stop the flow.

But Isaac dug **a third well,** and this time no spiders came, no enemies contended. He called it **Rehoboth,** saying, *"For now the Lord has made room for us, and we shall be fruitful in the land."*

Child of God, **keep digging.** Every seed you plant digs another well in your spiritual ground.

The first may be blocked. The second may be stolen. But the third will flow—and no spider will be able to stop it.

If you **kill this spider,** you will see your **Rehoboth** before the year is up. God has opened the way, but you must make room for your miracle. Your blessing is breaking through the ground—dig, expand, and step into what He has promised.. Your blessing is breaking through the ground.

Help me kill this spider—*not with rage, but with revelation.* **Because when this one dies, the whole web unravels.**

Help me kill this spider.

...

When the devourer is bound, the Recluse creeps in. It hides behind smiles and silence, feeding on offense, delay, and disappointment. Its venom is slow, secret, and spiritual—poisoning joy and paralyzing purpose. The Recluse thrives where pain is unspoken.

The Recluse Spider:
Poison in the Cracks of Complacency

The Recluse Spider is silent, secretive, and deadly. Unlike the flashy attacks of the Black Widow, this spider **works quietly in the shadows,** feeding on trust, patience, and time. It is **the master of isolation,** striking only after you

RECLUSE
SPIDER

have lowered your guard. It preys on leaders, families, and congregations, slowly **eroding unity and sowing confusion** without drawing attention to itself.

This spider **lurks in corners of your life you rarely examine**—in neglected relationships, unresolved conflict, or decisions postponed. It whispers subtly: *"It's not important now... wait... nobody will notice..."* and before you realize it, your spiritual life, your calling, or your church community has been compromised.

It is a spider of isolation. It leaves you feeling alone in your victories, disconnected from your calling, and unsure of what God has promised. You may not even recognize it until you glance around and see **how much it has quietly stolen**—dreams delayed, words left unsaid, opportunities passed over.

Imagine a woman in the church, faithful in her giving, diligent in prayer, yet always feeling a shadow over her ministry. She shares her vision, but opportunities seem to evaporate. Her words of encouragement to others are twisted into gossip. Doors she thought were open slammed shut. Slowly, almost imperceptibly, she begins to doubt herself, to question her calling, to wonder if God is really with her. This is the Recluse Spider at work—**quietly devouring life in places no one else sees.**

The Recluse Spider **devours opportunities to influence.** Vision becomes foggy, purpose feels delayed, and trust is broken. Like the Black Widow, it understands that **vision and leadership flow from the head**, but its method is patience, waiting for missteps to create gaps. The head of the house, the pastor, the ministry leader—anyone whose influence shapes others—is its target.

This spider feeds on **secrecy and neglect**. When conflicts go unaddressed, when prayer and vigilance are postponed, when accountability is ignored, the Recluse grows strong. Relationships fragment, unity fades, and the **enemy creeps into the church under the guise of small compromises.**

Scripture warns us of this quiet deception:

> *Be sober, be vigilant; because your adversary the devil, as a roaring lion, walketh about, seeking whom he may devour.*
>
> *1 Peter 5:8*

Though the lion roars, the Recluse doesn't roar—it hides, waiting until your defenses are down.

The **sign of the Recluse Spider** in your life is this: opportunities stall, relationships fracture subtly, and your spiritual walk feels "stuck" despite diligence. It can manifest as a slow financial drain, delayed answers to prayer, or persistent misunderstandings within your church.

But there is a strategy. **Faithful obedience, daily vigilance, and discerning community** expose this spider. Don't ignore small compromises—they are the cracks where it enters. Speak life over your relationships, your calling, and your family. Keep the channels of communication, prayer, and accountability open.

The Recluse Spider seems small, harmless, even invisible—but it **thrives in the cracks of complacency**. And yet, when your vigilance exposes it, when your light illuminates the hidden corners, its reign ends. The shadows cannot hold what is under God's authority.

The shadows tried to hold you captive—but your light just burned the Recluse Spider to ashes.

Help me kill this spider.

...

Once the hidden wounds are healed, the Black Widow emerges from the ruins. Her web is woven with fear, loneliness, and despair. She preys on the weary, those who have survived but stopped singing. Yet the light of Christ invades her darkness, and the joy of the Lord drives out every shadow.

The Black Widow Spider: Destroying Within

She is **the Black Widow.**

Her web is not spun in corners but in *covenants*. She builds in the sacred places—between hearts, within homes, inside marriages. When the enemy can no longer trap you through fear or lust, he sends this one—a spirit that destroys from within. Her venom doesn't enter through rebellion but through *relationship*. She weaves control into affection, deceit into devotion, until what was once *partnership becomes captivity*.

The **Black Widow** works quietly. She doesn't storm the door; she *studies patterns,* waiting for moments of weariness or disconnection. She thrives where communication breaks down, where wounds are left to fester instead of heal. Her mission is not simply to cause conflict—it is to *dismantle order*. For when divine order collapses, authority weakens, and the family loses its covering.

From the beginning, **vision has always flowed from the head.**

> *Where there is no vision, the people perish*
> *Proverbs 29:18*

God gave Adam the assignment, and Eve was designed as the divine counterpart—to incubate the seed and *multiply what God placed in him*. But when deception

BLACK WIDOW
SPIDER

entered, she began responding to the *whisper instead of the Word*. The enemy didn't need to overthrow Adam by force; he only had to confuse Eve's agreement. That same spirit of confusion still hunts today—*distorting trust, twisting truth, and turning covenant into competition.*

Once she mates, the **Black Widow kills her partner** and feeds him to her young. It's a horrifying image, yet it mirrors what happens in too many homes—when *words become weapons and love turns to bitterness.* A wife may never lift a hand, but through constant criticism, nagging, or belittling, she can drain her husband's strength until his spirit collapses. Children start to see their dad as inferior and immediately lose respect.

> *A foolish woman tears her house down with her own hands*
>
> *Proverbs 14:1*

But there is **another way.**

> *Death and life are in the power of the tongue*
>
> *Proverbs 18:21*

A *godly woman guards her mouth like a gate.* She knows her words build or break the man she loves. Her voice either *nurtures destiny* or *nourishes destruction.* When she speaks life, she becomes a weapon of restoration. Her words remind him of who he is in God. Her affection becomes strength; her honor becomes a source of strength; her faith becomes a source of fuel. She does not shrink in submission—she rises in wisdom, *aligning with divine design.*

God created man to **release**—to give, to protect, to provide—and woman to incubate and **multiply what she receives.** That's how *one seed can birth a nation.* Just as the Black Widow spins one sac that hatches a hundred spiders, so too does a woman carry within her the power to multiply what she releases. *Out of one womb can come one nation. Out of one heart can rise either a wicked generation or a righteous one.* Every word she speaks, every atmosphere she creates, becomes the web within which her children grow. She can act out of *wisdom or betrayal*—the choice determines what kind of legacy she births.

Remember the **mother of King Lemuel**, who spoke wisdom over her son in *Proverbs 31:2–3*:

> *What, my son? and what, the son of my womb? Give not thy strength unto women, nor thy ways to that which destroyeth kings.*

She understood the dangers of the Black Widow spirit and armed her son with discernment, teaching him how to survive in a venomous world.

Similarly, **Prince Agur's mother** guided him with insight, illustrating that godly women have the power to shape generations. As Prince Agur observed in Proverbs 30:24:

> *There be four things which are little upon the earth, but they are exceeding wise*

the ant, the coney, the locust, and the spider—he recognized that even the smallest can teach great lessons. These examples show that a mother's words, wisdom, and discernment are not incidental—they are foundational. Through her influence, she can protect her children from destruction or, if unwise, allow venom to take root. A single word can make or unmake a king.

A woman's wisdom doesn't stop in the nursery—it continues at the altar. The same discernment that guards her children also anchors her marriage. **Her voice carries weight—it can wound or it can water.** The enemy knows that if he can tangle communication between husband and wife, he can contaminate the entire house. That's why her words must **build, not bind; heal, not harm.**

But wisdom is more than words—it is watchfulness. A discerning woman doesn't just hear what her husband says; she senses what his silence means. She notices when his shoulders sink, when his laughter fades, when the weight of the world starts pressing down. **That's when she moves from speaking life to sustaining it.**

Think of it this way—a car doesn't apologize for needing fuel; it simply cannot move without it. When the tank runs low, the warning light flashes. **A wise wife sees those same signs in her husband—silence, frustration, fatigue—and instead of reacting, she refuels him with love, affirmation, and respect.** She doesn't do this out of obligation, but out of revelation: **she is his help meet, designed by God to complement, not compete.**

Every act of love is a declaration; every response becomes a prophecy. What you do speaks as loudly as what you say.

So guard your words, woman of God—but also your actions. *Your posture, your patience, your presence*—they all speak. What you speak is what your children will live, and what your husband will lead. Will you birth venom or virtue? Will your home multiply poison or purpose? The womb is sacred, the mouth is prophetic, and your influence can either build a legacy or breed destruction.

But God's work in the home was never meant to rest on one alone. **Marriage is sacred ground—a covenant where unity becomes warfare.** This is where spiritual harmony or discord is multiplied. The enemy watches for cracks—whispers, pride, and neglect—and will try to spin a web between husband and wife if they are not vigilant.

So husbands, your responsibility is to lead in love, covering and guiding your household with the same devotion Christ shows His Church.

> *And husbands, love your wives as Christ loved the Church*
>
> *Ephesians 5:25*

Ask her how she needs to be loved. Give her room to breathe and space to bloom. A wife is an **incubator**—whatever seed you plant in her, she multiplies. *Plant peace, reap harmony. Plant faith, reap power. Plant vision, reap legacy.*

When the husband leads in love and the wife speaks with wisdom, **heaven invades their home.** He is the *pastor of the house*—covering, protecting, and leading. She is the *prophet*—discerning, declaring, and shaping atmosphere. When the pastor and the prophet walk together, the home becomes a **sanctuary.**

> *A threefold cord is not quickly broken*
> *Ecclesiastes 4:12*

Be vigilant. Do not let the serpent convince you that the grass is greener elsewhere. There is no such thing as a *"work husband"* or *"work wife."* That's the whisper of the **Black Widow,** offering counterfeit comfort while weaving betrayal beneath the surface. **Stay alert, stay faithful, and stay submitted to God and to one another.**

Because **leadership in the kingdom begins at home.**

> *If a man cannot rule his own house, how shall he take care of the church of God?*
> *1 Timothy 3:5*

Before you pour into others, check your own covenant. *A home divided cannot host revival.*

So today, make a choice—

To build, *not to break.*

To speak life, *not death.*

To cherish, *not compete.*

To trust God in your spouse and honor the covenant He designed.

Together you will conquer.

Together you will prosper.

Together you will rise.

And your children will call you blessed.

Releasing Glory Over the Home

Father, we come boldly before Your throne in the Name of Jesus!

We thank You for Your Word, for Your wisdom, and for Your power that moves in covenant relationships.

Lord, we lift up every marriage here today. We lift up every husband and every wife. We break every web of the enemy—the Black Widow spirit, the deception, the control, the poison that seeks to destroy from within.

We speak life over every covenant. We speak restoration over every relationship. We speak vision over every home. Father, let

Your Spirit fall like rain! Let Your glory descend now!

Lord, we decree that every husband shall rise in love, leading with courage, patience, and protection. Let him walk in the fullness of his calling as the pastor of his home.

And Father, let every wife rise in wisdom, speaking life, nurturing faith, and multiplying purpose. Let her words be a fountain of blessing over her children, over her home, over her husband's destiny.

Father, we cancel every work of the enemy—every lie, every deception, every whispered thought of division, doubt, or betrayal. No more!

Lord, let the atmosphere in these homes be filled with Your peace. Let love, unity, and covenant order reign supreme. Let every seed sown in faith produce a harvest of blessing.

Father, we declare that the threefold cord is established—husband, wife, and God. Nothing can break it. No weapon formed against it shall prosper.

We decree that children will rise in the shadow of righteousness. Every word of life spoken by godly mothers shall multiply in their homes. Every instruction of wisdom shall protect against venom, against destruction, against the work of the enemy.

Lord, we release Your power. Heaven, move now. Let revival begin in these homes. Let Your glory fall. Let the blessings of

Abraham, Isaac, and Jacob be released over every marriage represented here today.

We declare that the enemy has no voice, no victory, no place. Father, fill these homes with Your joy, Your peace, Your provision, Your protection, Your presence.

We cover every covenant in the blood of Jesus. Every decision made in agreement with Your Word shall prosper. Every word spoken in faith shall bring life. Every home shall flourish.

Lord, we decree that love shall rule, faith shall reign, peace shall dwell, and vision shall guide. Let the enemy flee. Let every chain be broken. Let every high place be torn down.

Father, we call Heaven to rain down blessing upon every husband, every wife, every child. Let Your glory rest mightily upon these homes.

We thank You, Lord, for the victory that is already ours in Jesus' Name. Amen.

Lord, help me kill this spider.

...

After the devourer is bound, the Black Widow creeps in—the venom of hidden offense, delayed pain, and secret betrayal. Its bite goes unnoticed at first, but festers in the dark, poisoning joy and paralyzing purpose. This is the spider of silent suffering—the hidden wound that refuses to heal until it's exposed.

Fear is broken, but intimidation still breathes. Out from the shadows steps a giant—the Tarantula. It doesn't hide; it commands. It is the spirit of domination and control, seeking to rule the mind, silence the mouth, and crush the will. But this battle will end differently—the mind of Christ will triumph.

It is the **Tarantula**—the spirit of **intimidation, control, and domination**.

The Tarantula – The Battle of the Mind

Strength, when unguarded, is frightening. Samson didn't see the danger of being deceived while holding the power to crush his enemies. The **Tarantula**, though lethal, is also at risk if it misreads its environment or underestimates the subtle threat around it.

This is the terrifying truth: the most dangerous battles are often fought in the **mind**—where **deception, doubt**, and **distraction** can weaken even the strongest. Even the mightiest can be trapped by circumstances, temptation, or betrayal, when their focus wavers.

Shadows loom closer when **power is unaware**, and what is meant to be a **weapon for life** can easily become an **instrument of ruin**.

Samson lay his head in the lap of Delilah, a victim not of brute strength but of **deception and distraction**.

TARANTULA SPIDER

His strength alone could not save him when his **mind surrendered.**

The **mind unguarded is a battlefield.**

> *For as he thinketh in his heart, so is he.*
>
> *Proverbs 23:7*

> *Casting down imaginations, and every high thing that exalteth itself against the knowledge of God, and bringing into captivity every thought to the obedience of Christ.*
>
> *2 Corinthians 10:5*

The Tarantula's danger is not only in its fangs but in its **perception**; likewise, our own **power can become our prison** if our mind is compromised.

But this battle began long before Samson. It started in Heaven itself. Lucifer fell not by **force**, but by **thought**. The rebellion that split eternity was conceived in the **imagination of pride**.

> *For thou hast said in thine heart, I will ascend into heaven, I will exalt my throne above the stars of God... I will be like the Most High.*
>
> *Isaiah 14:13–14*

Notice those words: *"Thou hast said in thine heart."* Before there was war in Heaven, there was **war in the mind.**

Lucifer, adorned in beauty and anointed with glory, allowed **self-exaltation to cloud submission.** His focus shifted from the **Giver to the glory**, and what was once **light became darkness**. Even he who walked among the fiery stones stumbled when **pride whispered louder than obedience**.

This is why the **battle of the mind** is perhaps the most dangerous fight of all. Even the **strongest**, the **most gifted**, and the most powerful can fall if they do not guard their thoughts, measure their focus, and remain submitted to God.

Lucifer fell because he did not guard his thoughts; Samson fell because he did not guard his heart. Both prove that **strength without submission leads to destruction.**

Like the tarantula, we must **know our environment**, **trust our discernment**, and never underestimate the quiet, creeping dangers that lurk in the corners of the mind.

... *every* imagination must **bow.**

... *every* thought must **submit.**

> *Be transformed by the renewing of your mind.*
> *Romans 12:2*

Strength is not only in the hands or body—it is in the **clarity of thought**, the **alignment with God**, and the **ability to discern** the enemy's subtle attacks.

A **distracted or deceived mind** is as lethal as hidden fangs, ready to trap the unprepared.

Finally, brethren, whatsoever things are true, whatsoever things are honest, whatsoever things are just, whatsoever things are pure, whatsoever things are lovely, whatsoever things are of good report; if there be any virtue, and if there be any praise, think on these things.
Philippians 4:8

Help me kill this spider.

. . .

Do not allow **shadows of doubt or fear** to dictate your destiny. **Strength without vigilance can kill**, but strength under **God's guidance** conquers every enemy—visible and invisible.

Guard your mind, stay alert, and wield your power wisely—for your **mind determines** whether your strength becomes your **victory** or your **downfall**.

But take heart. Remember, **shadows can't kill**—they only provoke fear. The shadows cannot withstand the **light of obedience, faith, and vigilance**.

Yea, though I walk through the valley of the shadow of death, I will fear no evil: for Thou art with me; Thy rod and Thy staff they comfort me.
Psalm 23:4

Just as the spider spins her web, trying to trap and poison, every scheme of the enemy—every subtle snare, every hidden trap—is **already under your feet**.

> *The Lord is my light and my salvation; whom shall I fear? The Lord is the strength of my life; of whom shall I be afraid?*
>
> Psalm 27:1

Though the enemy sets his camp against you, though armies rise to challenge your peace, your **heart remains steadfast**, your **confidence anchored in Him**.

The **expected end that** God promised—the *room, the breakthrough, the divine expansion*—is ready for you. Your vision is not stalled; it is **brewing in the unseen**, waiting for the moment God commands it to burst forth.

Doors that seemed closed are already swinging wide.

Relationships once frayed are being restored.

The **purpose** planted in your heart is undeniable and unstoppable.

The enemy may whisper **delay, despair, and doubt**, but your faith will **roar life, breakthrough, and multiplication**.

Your **light is too bright**, your **seed too fertile**, your **destiny too divine** to be held back.

Stand firm, shine boldly, and watch as **God turns every shadow**, every web the enemy spins, into a **stage for your victory**.

The spiders tried to claim your vision, your harvest, your purpose—but **God's light is stronger**. Stand now in **authority**, step into your **purpose**, and watch every hidden snare **crumble beneath your feet.**

Victory is not coming—it is already here.

Help me kill these spiders.

The Declaration of Deliverance: Breaking the Spider's Grip

Father, in the mighty name of Jesus, we come standing in authority and covered by Your blood.

*We thank You that **every spider exposed in this chapter**—the Loxosceles, the Wolf, the Hopping, the Hati Hati, the Two-Faced, the Trap-Door, the Recluse, the Black Widow, and the Tarantula—**is now under our feet.** The web is breaking, the curse is lifting, and the power of deception is destroyed.*

*__Lord, we renounce every ditch dug for our downfall.__ What was meant for evil, You have already turned for good. Like Joseph, we declare: "You meant it for harm, but God meant it for my saving." We will not die in the pit—we will rise from it. **Every pit, every prison, every plan of the enemy is reversed in Jesus' name.***

*__Father, we silence the voice of the Wolf Spider__—the false prophet, the seducer, the manipulator. Every spirit that comes disguised in light but carries darkness, **we expose and expel by the power of the Holy Ghost.** Every counterfeit voice that sought to charm, confuse, or devour Your people—**we command it to flee now!** Let truth pierce deception, and let purity cleanse Your house.*

__We cast down the Hopping Spider__—every transference of demonic influence, every unholy laying on of hands. Father, give us discernment in this hour. Let our spirits recognize contamination before it takes root. Just as the blood of Jesus covered us during the plague, let **Your covering rest upon us, our homes, and our families.** No spirit shall hop from post to post, pew to pew, or hand to hand—the bloodline is drawn!

We crush the Hati Hati Spider—the shallow praise that depends on prosperity. Lord, **we will praise You when the account is low, when the car is gone, when the cupboards are bare.** Our worship will not waver with our wallet. **You are still God, and You are still good.**

We drive out the Two-Faced Spirit—the unstable, the double-minded, the deceptive heart. Create in us clean hearts, O God, and renew right spirits within us. **Purge the chameleons from our circle.** Expose every tongue that flatters in public but poisons in private.

We close the mouth of the Trap-Door Spider—the devourer of finances and fruit. Every leech spirit that eats away at what we earn, **we bind it in Jesus' name.** Every devouring locust, every hidden hole where blessings leak out—be sealed by the anointing. **Lord, rebuke the devourer for our sake!**

We discern and defeat the Recluse Spider—the venom of hidden offense, delayed pain, and dangerous associations. Heal us from the invisible bites that fester later. **Expose every secret wound, every unspoken betrayal, every subtle bitterness that tries to eat away at our joy.** We choose freedom over infection!

We confront the Black Widow—the spirit of fear, loneliness, and despair. You shall not weave your web in our minds or our homes. **We declare the joy of the Lord is our strength.** The depression lifts, the fear breaks, the loneliness dissolves. **The light of Christ floods every shadow, every corner, every palace of our lives.**

And now, Father, we face the Tarantula—the battle of the mind. **Every thought not aligned with Your Word, we bring into captivity to the obedience of Christ.** We tear down imaginations that exalt themselves against the knowledge of God. **Pride, doubt, distraction, and confusion—your web is broken!** Lord, renew our minds daily. **Let every thought, every plan, every meditation be pure, righteous, and anchored in truth.** We will think as Heaven thinks, see as Heaven sees, and walk in perfect peace.

Now, Father, we put on the whole armor of God—the belt of truth, the breastplate of righteousness, the shield of faith, and the sword of the Spirit. **We stand firm in Your power, not our own.** The atmosphere shifts. The cobwebs burn. The spiders scatter. The house is swept clean and filled with glory.

This is our declaration: *The curse is broken. The anointing flows. The oil is fresh. The fire is hot. The palace is clean. The web is gone.* **We are free indeed!**

In the mighty, matchless name of Jesus Christ— **Amen and Amen!**

TESTIMONY

AND THEY OVERCAME HIM BY THE BLOOD OF THE LAMB,
AND BY THE WORD OF THEIR TESTIMONY
REVELATION 12:11

Chapter 7

My Testimony

And they overcame him by the blood of the Lamb, and by the word of their testimony; and they loved not their lives unto the death..

Revelation 12:11

I want to conclude by saying this — it is vital for you, the reader of this book, to understand that **I myself had the fight of my life** getting out of a spider's web. I was bitten by a spider called **pride**.

At the height of my ministerial success — making close to one million dollars a year, pastoring two churches at the same time with jam-packed congregations, preaching all over the world — **I was bitten by that same spider called pride.**

> *Pride goeth before destruction, and a haughty spirit before a fall.*
>
> Proverbs 16:18

Around 2002, I found myself **losing everything I had** — financial success, ministry influence, and even my marriage. I had to come to the hard conclusion that I was caught in **the web of pride, and it was no one's fault but my own.**

At my lowest point, I stopped preaching for six months. I ignored the calls for revival, avoided the pulpits that once welcomed me, and hid behind shame and silence.

But one man — one true friend — saw through the spider's web and came to my rescue. That man was **Bishop Lambert Wade Gates.**

He had been looking for me because he wanted me to preach at a tent revival in Indianapolis, but I didn't answer his calls. I didn't feel worthy to preach anymore. The spider's web had trapped me.

Somehow, he found me while he was at a Tri-State Convention. He put me in his car, drove me to a hotel, and said, "Tonight, you will preach in my stead."

I looked at him and said, "Man, you're crazy. I haven't preached in six months."

To this day, I have no idea how he found me — I was in Columbus, Ohio, and somehow ended up in Indianapolis, standing in a hotel room, changing clothes I didn't even own. Bishop Gates handed me **a pair of black pants and a white shirt** and said, "Let's go to church."

We went to **Christ Church**, where **Bishop Shawn Tyson's father** was the pastor. Over **2,000 people** attended that night.

Bishop Gates dropped me off at the back of the church, where Bishop Shawn Tyson met me at the door and embraced me. Crying and trembling, I felt completely inadequate to stand before God's people. But Bishop Gates insisted — he pushed me toward that platform.

He grabbed me by the chest and said, **"Calm yourself — you're preaching tonight."**

When I entered the sanctuary and stepped onto the platform, I saw thousands of familiar faces looking at me. My body was shaking. Then the **Holy Spirit** whispered, *"Don't look at their faces."*

Bishop Tyson laid his hand on my knee and said, **"Be still — you're up next."**

I walked slowly to the podium. It felt like I took a thousand steps to get there. With a trembling voice, I opened my Bible to the **Book of Judges** — the story of **Jephthah**, the son who was rejected because he was born illegitimately.

That night, I preached from this thought: **"If you drop me, I'll land on my feet."**

And when I released that word — the spider webs **broke**, the **fire fell**, the **oil began to flow**, and the people began to **dance before the Lord.**

The glory cloud filled the house. I laid the microphone down gently and returned to my seat, but the power of God continued to move. I didn't need to preach another word — **I was delivered that night.**

Over **100 people** came to the altar for deliverance, and around **70 were baptized in Jesus' name.** That was a Friday night. Bishop Gates made me stay and preach **three more times** that weekend.

When we left there, we went straight to **Louisville, Kentucky**, with **Bishop Michael Ford Sr.**, and from that time until now — **every spider has been killed in my life.**

And I can genuinely say, through **George Dawson Ministries**, in my lifetime of preaching, **over one million souls** have been brought into the Kingdom of God.

So you see, my friend...

Never mind the cobwebs — just keep killing those spiders.

> *The righteous cry, and the Lord heareth, and delivereth them out of all their troubles.*
>
> *Psalm 34:17*

Even after all I went through, I found out that **God still hears.** He heard me on the web. He heard me in the fall. He heard me in the silence. And just like He heard me, He's hearing you right now. The same God that restored me is the same God who will restore you. **He is still Jehovah Rapha — the Lord that healeth thee** (*Exodus 15:26*).

When your soul is weary and your strength is gone, remember this:

> *He restoreth my soul; He leadeth me in paths of righteousness for His name's sake*
>
> *Psalm 23:3*

God is not just repairing you — He's renewing you.

> *Behold, I will do a new thing; now it shall spring forth*
>
> *Isaiah 43:19*

You don't have to live bound, tangled, or trapped anymore.

The Word declares,

> *Stand fast therefore in the liberty wherewith Christ hath made us free*
>
> *Galatians 5:1*
>
> *if the Son therefore shall make you free, ye shall be free indeed*
>
> *John 8:36*

You are not who you used to be. The web does not define you — **the Word defines you.**

Even in our failures, **His love never lets go.**

Yea, I have loved thee with an everlasting love: therefore with lovingkindness have I drawn thee

Jeremiah 31:3

That's the kind of love that reaches into dark places and pulls you out with power. That's the kind of love that heals what was broken and breathes life back into dry places.

Now, as we prepare to pray, I want you to believe that every word that leaves your mouth carries authority. Heaven is responding. The same God who heard my cry and delivered me **is hearing yours right now.**

Declaration of Freedom

*Father, in the name of Jesus, we come before You with power and authority, praying the Mind of God — that **Your will be done on Earth as it is in Heaven**, that our expected end will come forth in full.*

*We **command the devil right now**: put back everything you've attempted to steal — **our minds, our peace, our love, our joy** — put it back **with interest!** We didn't give it to you; you took it without permission. But now, **we serve you notice** — your time is up. WE command that everything that is ours is put back in the name of Jesus.*

No more!
No more dead flies in our oil.
No more webs.
No more spiders.
No more entanglements.

*We declare that **we have the authority**, and you are **subject to our jurisdiction**. Every witch, every warlock, every seducing spirit — we sever every tie right now in the name of Jesus. We **close every entrance** that's been opened in our lives.*

*God, **smite the enemy with blindness!** Let the **light of Jesus Christ** shine so bright in us that the enemy cannot see to size us up. We rebuke every form of demonic surveillance —*

every spirit trying to monitor, mimic, or study our movements — and we declare, **The devil is a liar!**

According to **Psalm 91**, *He that dwelleth in the secret place of the Most High shall abide under the shadow of the Almighty.*

No more infringement in our secret place — enemy, you are trespassing! Every door opened by principalities, powers, and rulers of darkness in these regions is **closed and locked now** in the name of Jesus.

Lord, **calibrate us** — calibrate our ears, calibrate our eyes. Tune our discernment to Heaven's frequency. We even forbid the enemy to speak our names! We snatch our names out of the mouths of evil right now. Just like You did at Babel, Lord — **confuse their language**. Let every demonic conversation about us be scattered and silenced in Jesus' name.

We thank You for **the oil** that repels serpents, that **forbids the leviathan and the python** from sizing us up to choke the life out of us. We thank You for **the oil without dead flies**, and the **blood of Jesus** that puts us in right standing with God.

We thank You for **the fire** — **the hot fire** — the fire that causes Jesus to walk with us, just like **Shadrach, Meshach, and Abednego**. When the fire was turned up seven times hotter, the same fire that killed their enemies set them free. This is same fire you walked with them in. Lord, **let that fire burn bright in us!** Let it cause the fresh oil to rise as a sweet-smelling savor before You.

*We come against **every Jezebel spirit** that seeks to usurp Your prophets, and **every Delilah** that seeks to seduce Your sons into surrendering their strength. We come against **every witch, warlock, voodoo, and hoodoo spirits**, and every demonic influence trying to prevent destiny from coming forth.*

*By the authority of **Jesus Christ**, we declare:*

Your hold is broken.

Your web is destroyed.

Your grip is gone.

*We declare that **we are healed**, we are **delivered**, and we are **free** in the name of Jesus!*

Lord, forgive us for every time we gave the enemy access. Forgive us for every moment we became the web in someone else's life. Forgive us for being the spider in another person's story. We humble ourselves before You, Lord, and we repent for every dead fly we've allowed in our oil.

Heal those we have hurt with our words, our actions, and our attitudes. Thank you for giving us another opportunity to get it right. Thank You for the mercy that meets us anew every morning.

*We also thank You for the gift of **forgiveness**. Thank You for every spider, every web, every snake that crossed our path — not because we welcome them, but because **they revealed Your*** *power* to deliver us. *What the enemy meant for evil,* **You turned for good.**

Lord, we thank You that **the bite didn't kill us**, and **the snake didn't choke the life out of us.** *We pray deliverance over those who are still entangled — set them free in the name of Jesus! Heal the minds that have been poisoned by venom.* **Cleanse the blood, purify the thoughts, restore the peace!**

We thank You for right minds, for sweet sleep, and for peace that passes understanding. No more restless nights because of the pain of the bite — the venom is released, and **we are healed!**

Everywhere the soles of our feet tread, **we shall possess the land.** *We walk in victory.* **The foundations are moving on our behalf!**

We thank You, Lord, for **renewed vision**, *renewed obedience, and a skillful prayer life. We give You all the glory, all the honor, and all the praise.*

For You alone are worthy. You alone are holy. You alone are mighty to save.

And today, we declare together —

No more webs.

No more Spiders.

Only fire, only oil, only Jesus.

In the mighty name of Jesus,

Amen and Amen.

We believe this book is not just a message — it's a movement. It will spark deliverance, ignite freedom, and awaken purpose in the lives of God's people. As your faith rises and your testimony unfolds, we would love to hear what the Lord has done for you through this word. Your story will strengthen others and glorify God's power. Please share your testimony by writing to us at **dnjgoree@sundaymorningministries.org**. Together, let's celebrate the goodness, the power, and the delivering hand of our God.

If the Lord has touched your life through the pages of this book and you feel led to sow a seed of thanksgiving and deliverance, we invite you to do so in faith. Every seed sown helps us continue sharing the gospel of freedom and healing to those still entangled in the web. You may send your seed to

Cash App: $GeorgeDawson

We thank you for your love, your prayers, and your obedience to the leading of the Holy Spirit.

www.ingramcontent.com/pod-product-compliance
Lightning Source LLC
Chambersburg PA
CBHW072050290426
44110CB00014B/1628